TREASURE KIDS

50 ***True*** **Stories on**
Real **Kids Finding** ***Real*** **Treasure**

Jack Myers

Treasure Kids

A Jack O'Lantern Press book

© 2017 by Jack Myers

ISBN: 9781981339785

First edition: 2017

All rights reserved. No part of this book may be reproduced in any form or any electronic, mechanical, or other means now known or hereafter invented, including photocopying or recording, or stored in any information storage or retrieval systems without the express written permission of the publisher, except for newspaper, magazine, or other reviewers who wish to quote brief passages in connection with a review.

This book is an original publication of Jack O'Lantern Press.

Jack O'Lantern Press
For inquiries: jackmyers@peoplepc.com

To
Cecelia Reihl,
for her patience over the years in the researching and writing of my unusual books,
and

to
Pat and Jack Myers, my parents.

Table of Contents

Introduction

Illustration by N.C. Wyeth

"Fifteen men on the dead man's chest — ho-ho and a bottle of rum!"

Who could ever forget the magical, wonderful 1883 novel ***Treasure Island***? It is perhaps the greatest adventure story ever told, a classic pirates' tale about a young boy caught up in a dramatic, danger-filled hunt for buried gold — across the high seas on a faraway tropical island. ***Treasure Island*** boasts bigger than life characters — memorable adventurers such as young Jim Hawkins, Billy Bones, Benn Gunn, and the immortal specter of a one-legged pirate named Long John Silver — with that ever-present parrot perched forever on his buccaneer shoulder. Author Robert Louis Stevenson gave the world the very caricature of pirate with his invention of the brave, smooth-talking, but ultimately treacherous Silver.

But no matter how charming and thrilling, ***Treasure Island*** was never more than an imaginary, clever piece of make-believe fiction. Young Jim Hawkins never existed. There was no Billy Bones, Benn Gunn, or even the legendary Long John Silver with that pegged leg.

There really never was any Treasure Island.

But treasures *do* exist. They exist along with the people who find them. And some of the most astounding treasures discovered to date have been recovered by kids. Meteorites, fossilized dinosaur bones, ancient artifacts, bags of stolen loot, wads of lost cash, pots of buried coins, shiny gold nuggets, precious gemstones, unknown insects . . . why, a girl in upstate New York even found her very own undiscovered supernova!

Kids have sharp eyes, a keen sense of adventure, and, unlike grownups, don't usually stay on the beaten path.

Kids have a nose for treasure and a need for action. . . .

So, welcome to ***Treasure Kids!*** . . . 50 true stories about real everyday kids discovering honest-to-goodness authentic valuable treasure. The kind of treasure that makes headlines!

We give you ***Treasure Kids!*** where each story has a different twist, every treasure is unique, and all 50 discoveries can be described as the finds of a lifetime. . . .

Treasure Kids!

Source: National Park Service

Source: *Tampa Bay Times*

Chapter 1 ♦ We're in the Money!

Although treasure comes in many varied forms — and this book certainly proves that — nothing is better or more exciting than finding good, old, hard cash. That is, real MONEY . . . and in the very first chapter, our treasure kids definitely finds lots and lots of it!

So, let the treasure discoveries begin. . . .

Legend of the Lost Union Payroll

In the spring of 1902, a trio of country boys went exploring the woods just east of Rogersville, Tennessee. Young Bobby Venable was accompanied by his friends John and Taylor, who are today known only by their first names. A severe storm had recently blown through the Rogersville area, damaging houses and knocking over several trees. Bobby spotted an a partially uprooted tree, with its spider web of roots yanked out of the ground creating a small, black hole underneath. John figured this might be a good place for rabbits to hide, and knelt down to reach down inside the recently formed cavity. However, instead of coming out with the anticipated fistful of fur, the country boy instead pulled out a fistful of shiny silver dollars.

Elated, the boys began excavating the hole and filling their trousers with the big, silver coins. They took what they could carry, then returned with a shovel to dig for more.

In all, it was reported that the boys recovered an impressive total of $1,512 in silver coinage, most which had been contained in a metal cooking pot. The parents of Bobby, John, and Taylor insisted the trio report their find to the local authorities, which they did. The local officials made an attempt to find the rightful owner of the coins, but proved unable to do so.

Meanwhile, Tennessee newspapers caught wind of the story. Eventually news of the find spread nationwide.

Many months later, a letter was delivered to Rogersville addressed to Bobby Venable. The letter sported a New York City postmark, and was written by a now elderly gentleman who claimed to have served during the Civil War as a corporal in the Union Army. According to this New Yorker, he was assigned to escort a large payroll shipment of silver coins destined for fellow Union soldiers stationed near the border of Tennessee and North Carolina (to the east of Rogersville). However, as the shipment neared Big Creek, only 20 miles south from the Virginia border, the soldiers guarding the payroll came under heavy attack from Confederate forces. At the beginning of the fierce battle, a Union captain ordered the corporal to assist him in hastily burying the payroll and other critical supplies at the bases of nearby trees. As the pair went from tree to tree, the battle moved closer. Suddenly, the captain was shot dead, and the corporal ran for his life through the woods, eventually coming to a farmhouse where the farmer and his wife gave him shelter. Ultimately, the corporal defected from his unit, returning home to New York City where he hid from government officials for many years, fearing arrest.

In a subsequent letter to Bobby Venable, the writer particularly described grabbing several sacks with coins and stuffing those sacks into a large, heavy kettle, which he then quickly buried beneath a tree. The former Union corporal said he did not know Big Creek and the Rogersville area, had only been there on the day of the attack, and was confused as to the exact location of the treasure. He confessed to having always been uncomfortable about returning to Rogersville to look for the buried payroll. The Northerner was well aware of the animosity that Southerners still held for Yankees such as himself — especially those who had soldiered in the much-hated Union Army.

News of the Yankee's letter soon leaked out in Rogersville, and within no time the woods near this sleepy Southern town became filled with fortune hunters furiously digging holes. Did anyone ever find anything? No finds were ever *officially* reported. What is known is that the Yankee letter-writer claimed that sacks of silver coins were buried in about a dozen locations in those woods. So, we are left with four possibilities, treasure kids.

First, the letter writer from New York was a prankster. However, the author did reveal his knowledge about coins being buried inside a cooking pot. And the letters to Bobby Venable reportedly seemed authentic and genuine.

Second, the Confederate soldiers who won the Battle of Big Creek somehow found out about the hurriedly buried payroll and were successful in recovering all the freshly buried payroll sacks.

Third, the treasure hunters who dug up the woods after Bobby Venerable discovery and subsequent letter from New York City were able to recover the rest of the silver — but declined to tell anyone.

And fourth, the remainder of the buried payroll of silver coins is still out there, waiting to be uncovered.

Rogersville is located on U.S. Highway 11W in the northeastern corner of Tennessee, within easy driving distance of Virginia, Kentucky, and North Carolina. In many fairy tales, a pot of gold is said to wait at the other end of the rainbow. But for young Bobby Venable and his pals, a pot of more than 1500 silver dollars revealed itself almost magically after a severe spring thunderstorm uprooted a tree in the nearby forest. Only the boys' leprechaun proved to be a badly frightened Union soldier, in fear for his life, running from a bloody Civil War battle some 40 years prior.

Kids Bring Home $98,000 in Mysterious Duffel Bag

Some kids playing in a field just east of Boulder, Colorado in early 2005 made a startling discovery. The children found a duffel bag crammed with approximately **$98,000** in cold, hard cash. The kids promptly handed over the bag containing the loot to local cops.

Police believed the bag is related to a criminal drug case from 2002, but had a hard time proving it. The mysterious bag had obviously been sitting outside for some time, and the money was very wet and moldy. The way the money was packaged made the police suspicious that it was connected to the illegal sale of drugs. It took technicians working for the police hours to dry and separate the old bills, many of which had become stuck together and were very fragile.

Because of the suspicious nature of this case, the parents of the kids have requested that authorities not release their names or ages. We don't even know if these are boys or girls who found the money. Although the exact location of the discovery was not released, we know that the money bag was found somewhere near the vicinity of Fairview Rd. and North 76th Street, less than a mile east of the Base Line Reservoir.

Treasure Kids!

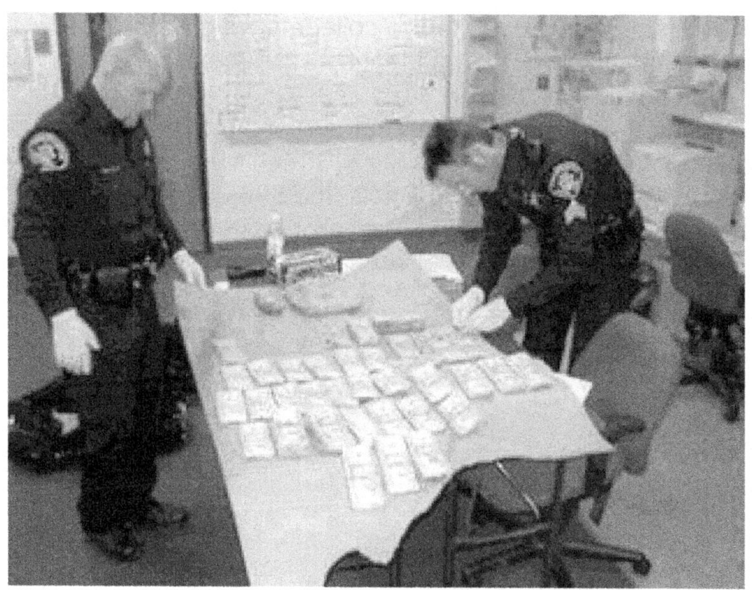

The kids and their families were told that if no one stepped forward to claim the money within 90 days, they, as finders of the money, would be allowed to keep it. However, the money was not released to the families after 90 days because investigators were still trying to link the stash to past illegal drug activity. In such cases, if the police can prove a connection to a criminal case, it would be up to a judge to decide what happens to the money.

The FBI and Secret Service were called in to assist with the investigation. However, with no hard evidence linking the money to a specific crime or ongoing case, the money was eventually released to the three Boulder County kids who found it. Reportedly, the loot was evenly divided, with parents of the three minors being presented with checks from the sheriff's office for their kids' share of the dough. Most of the actual paper money recovered was too old to be put back in circulation and had to be destroyed.

"It's a pretty good start to college savings," said one mom who asked not to be identified, "so the children are happy about that."

And so, we bet, are the mothers and the fathers! Good colleges are far from cheap.

According to county officials, the $98,000 represented the largest amount of money ever found in Boulder — and turned in.

Israeli Boy Unearths Coin Described in Bible

In the Bible's book of Exodus, it is commanded that every Jew, regardless of their station in life, contribute a ***half-shekel coin*** each year to the Temple. The Temple, of course, once stood on the Temple Mount, the main religious site in the Old City of Jerusalem. The Temple was a place where, for centuries, Jewish pilgrims flocked for religious feasts. Judaism considers the Temple Mount to be the spot where God chose the Divine Presence to rest. Also known as Mount Moriah, it is believed to be where God gathered the dust to create the first man on earth, Adam. Muslims call it the "Noble Sanctuary," and believe the Temple Mount to be the location from which the prophet Muhammad ascended to heaven. It is a piece of holy land of extreme importance to Jews, Christians, and Muslims alike.

Several years ago, Muslim authorities in charge of the Temple Mount compound removed large quantities of dirt during a construction project, and moved that considerable debris to another location. The Israelis were not happy about what the Muslims did, but made the best of the circumstances. They assembled an amazing volunteer staff of some 40,000 people (enough to fill many Major League baseball stadiums) to sift through the ancient dirt, combing through the dusty piles to look for priceless historical artifacts.

In 2008, a 14-year old Israeli boy named Omri Ya'ari discovered the first silver half-shekel coin known to originate from the Temple itself. The coin, minted during the 66-67 A.D. so-called "Great Revolt" against the Romans, is considered to be an extremely rare find in Jerusalem. It was probably used to pay Temple taxes, as described in the Bible, and shows some fire damage. That damage is likely the result of the Romans having destroyed the Second Temple in 70 A.D. This was the Romans' was of trying to put down the Jewish uprising against Roman rule (they, in fact, destroyed large portions of Jerusalem). The first, original Temple, built by Solomon (son of David) in 957 B.C., was destroyed way back in 516 B.C. by the Babylonians. The Muslim Al Aqsa Mosque (built 720 A.D.) and Dome of the Rock (built 691 A.D. on the rock from which Muhammad is said to have ascended) today occupy the approximate location of the original first and second Temple from Biblical times.

The half-shekel coin found by 14-year old Omri would have been minted on site at the Temple. It is well-preserved despite evidence of having gone through the 70 A.D. fire, just three-four years after the coin was struck. The face of the coin clearly shows a branch of three pomegranates, along with the ancient Hebrew letters that spell out "HOLY JERUSALEM." The flip side or "obverse" clearly spells out "half shekel" and also depicts a chalice.

So far, some 3,500 coins have been found in this treasured mountain of ancient soil, including coins from the recent Ottoman era of less than 100 years ago, and going as far back as the distant era of Persian rule in Israel — hundreds of years B.C.

No coin has proven more important, however, than the much-celebrated silver half-shekel discovered by 14-year old Omri Ya'ari. It is a 2,000-year old Biblical artifact minted at the Temple, buried at the same Temple for all these centuries, and ultimately unearthed from Temple Mount soil by this young Israeli who volunteered his time like so many others. Volunteers who only wished to preserve history.

To Omri and all others who have helped, we say "Mazel tov!"

Congratulations, Omri.

Ohio Boys Chase Snakes, Find Cash Instead

A couple of 14-year old boys searching for garter snakes in 1951 stumbled upon a pile of cash beyond their wildest dreams. Mike Riegler and Billy Wigley were busy catching snakes one fine April day in Akron, Ohio when the duo decided to grab a tin can in which to stash their slippery reptiles. While rooting through a pile of leaves and trash in a nearby field, Billy Wigley kicked over a likely snake can. But wait a minute, there beside the can, poking out from under some leaves, lay an old, torn $50 bill.

Gadzooks!

Mike and Billy quickly snatched up the $50 and began searching excitedly for more money. Snakes could certainly wait for another day.

To the pair's amazement, more fifties began popping out of the rubbish pile, along with some torn and tattered 20s. Inside of an hour, the boys had collected some 55 old and moldy dead presidents totaling $1,400. Not a bad haul even by 2010 standards, this was a positive treasure trove in 1951. With nearly 60 years of inflation that $1,400 would equal close to $15,000 in today's world.

Only one problem, the boys weren't convinced the money was real. What if it were funny money — fake money dumped by some shady counterfeiter? Rotting money that was, in fact, just plain rotten? Mike and Billy suddenly had their doubts.

Since Billy's dad was in the banking business, the boys decided to take their find to Mr. Wigley. However, Mr. Wigley, the assistant secretary for the local Dime Bank, examined the old currency and very quickly pronounced it genuine. None of the bills were dated later than 1934, raising suspicion the bills had possibly sat under that heap of rubbish for quite some time.

Unfortunately, Mr. Wigley had a quite different unpleasant surprise for the boys. The banker insisted on calling the police, although Mike and Billy had been more in favor of a "finders keepers" policy towards their recovered stash.

Well, the cops came and took the boys' big find, promising that if no one came forward within 30 days, the money would belong to the boys.

The next day, the police wisely did their own search of the trash pile and came up with an extra $200 that Mike and Billy had, in their haste, overlooked. The police wanted to deposit the cash in their pension fund, but reporters from the *Akron Beacon Journal* newspaper convinced the cops to add it to the $1,400 already recovered by Mike and Billy.

Meanwhile, as news of the discovery hit the pages of the *Beacon Journal*, rumors began to fly all around town. Who had dumped all that money in an abandoned lot? Robbers? Gangsters? An eccentric millionaire?

It would be a very long 30-day waiting period for the cautiously hopeful boys.

The year before, an Akron woman had the misfortune of having more than $1,000 in cash stolen during a burglary of her home. Naturally, the victim applied for the money found in the trash pile, hoping it might be hers. However, the denominations stolen from the lady's house didn't match Mike and Billy's discovery, which happened to contain all 50s and 20s. So, the woman's claim for the cash was denied.

The cops warned that whoever legitimately came forward with a claim on the $1,600 was probably going to be hit with a hefty fine for littering, since the field off Mull Avenue was an illegal dumping ground. It seems the police themselves were now pulling for Mike and Billy to keep all the mystery money.

Finally, on May 29th, 1951, Mike and Billy were summoned to the office of the Akron police chief. There, the boys were awarded the entire $1,600 . . . to be split 50/50. Payment came in the form of crisp, new bills — the money the boys had recovered was hardly fit for circulation, and was scheduled to be destroyed after first being sent to Washington, D.C. The boys' parents put away most of the brand spanking new cash for future educational expenses. The big spending spree Mike and Billy had dreamed of for weeks never actually did happen.

No one ever conclusively figured out from where the discarded old money had come. As an adult, Mike Riegler offered perhaps the most likely explanation. Mr. Riegler theorized that someone had stashed the money in old newspapers for safekeeping, and then for whatever reason, those papers had been accidentally dumped into that vacant West Akron lot.

No robbers, no gangsters, just someone's very costly, extremely expensive mistake.

But why then did the owner never come back to pick up the lost cash? Mike and Billy were able to scoop up almost all the loot in a matter of minutes — once they had successfully uncovered the location of the treasure.

Treasure Kids!

The answer to this puzzle will likely never be known. What is known is that, bottom line, the situation turned out *finders keepers* for treasure kids Mike Riegler and Billy Wigley of Akron, Ohio.

Boy Finds Rare Penny Worth $72,500!

A sharp-eyed 14-year old boy from Long Beach, California found one of the rarest, most highly sought-after coins known to coin collectors. And how did he do it? By checking his pocket change, and by asking his parents to get rolls of pennies from the bank so he could check them. Kenneth Wing, an avid young coin collector, had made it his goal to collect Lincoln cents from every year (going back to 1909) and from every U.S. Mint (Philadelphia, Denver, and San Francisco).

The unusual coin that Kenneth found as a boy in 1944 was the then unheard of 1943-S copper penny (**S** being for San Francisco). Sounds pretty ordinary, right? Except that in 1943, the United States Mint supposedly produced *only* steel pennies that were coated in zinc with a distinctive milky-gray color. The year 1943 was at the height of World War II, and the U.S. Government badly needed extra copper supplies for the war effort. So, instead of making the familiar Lincoln cents from the usual brown copper, an entire year's supply of cents (over a billion) was made from zinc-coated gray steel. These "steel" pennies have long since been highly prized by collectors.

But there weren't supposed to be *any* 1943 copper cents. None! Yet young coin collector Kenneth Wing from

Long beach insisted he had found one. Kenneth took the penny to a local coin dealer, who immediately offered the boy $500 for it (or, 50,000 pennies for a single Lincoln cent). Kenneth turned down the dealer's offer to buy his unusual coin.

In 1946, the Wing Family wrote to the acting director of the U.S. Mint, Leland Howard, asking about Kenneth's 1943-S copper penny. The director wrote back that "*In reference to your letter of August 11th, there were no copper cents struck during the calendar year 1943 at any of the coinage Mints. Only the zinc coated steel cent was struck during that year.*"

Officially, Kenneth's 1943 copper penny didn't exist!

But in 1948, Kenneth and family showed the 1943 copper penny to the director of the San Francisco Mint. It was the mint executive's private opinion that Kenneth's rare find was genuine. In 1957, Kenneth' father contacted the U.S. Treasury Department for verification. However, the U.S. Treasury instead referred the Wings to the Smithsonian Institution in Washington, D.C.

In June 1957, experts at the Smithsonian pronounced that, in their learned opinion, the Kenneth Wing 1943-S copper cent was genuine. One of the simple tests performed on the coin was the magnet test. Steel is magnetic, while copper is not.

For the rest of his life until his passing in 1996, Kenneth Wing remained a coin collector. But he never did part with his prized 1943-S copper cent. Instead, Kenneth kept the prized coin under lock-and-key in a safe deposit box, rarely showing it to anyone.

Upon Wing's death in 1996, Wing's heirs contacted Steven Contursi of Rare Coin Wholesalers to have the 1943 copper cent authenticated. Not only did Contursi authenticate the cent, but he also struck a deal to buy the penny from the Wing family for $72,500! That's seven million, two-hundred and fifty thousand pennies if you do the math.

Think Mr. Contursi paid too much? The coin dealer later sold the coin to another collector at a much higher, undisclosed price. Rumors have placed this second sale at $150,000 . . . yes, 15 million pennies in exchange for a single red cent. A 1943 red cent, that is.

Over the years, a handful of other 1943 copper pennies have surfaced (some from the Philadelphia and Denver, and not just the San Francisco Mint). The most likely explanation is that a few copper blanks (known as planchets) from 1942 got stuck in the mint machines, and then got unstuck during the 1943 minting process and got struck along with the 1943 steel cents. This also explains why a small handful of 1944 steel pennies were also found. Steel blanks became stuck in the machines during 1943, then fell out and were struck along with the 1944 copper cents (the mints had returned to using copper in 1944).

Does the U.S. Mint still make errors? Yes! And do collectors still pay big bucks for coins with these errors? Absolutely! One easy to spot error is on the Washington and Sacagawea dollar coins. If you find a dollar coin with one side blank (known as an unburnished planchet), you are looking at a dollar coin that can be sold to a collector for as much as $1,000! Coins with mistakes are hard to find as the U.S. Mint tries very hard to prevent these mistakes from happening. But, as 14-year old Kenneth Wing proved, mistakes do happen. And when mistakes happen, sharp-eyed coin collectors can cash in big!

Viking Coin Hoard Unearthed by Nine-year Old Boy

In the spring of 2008, nine-year old Alexander Granhof and his grandfather, Jens Granhof, decided to go looking for treasure. But, it wasn't the kind of treasure you would expect. In 1676, the historic Battle of Lund had taken place just outside of what is today the City of Lund in southern Sweden. Since Alexander and his grandfather lived nearby, they hoped to search the site of the old battlefield in hopes of finding a 17th-century cannonball — or even just a piece of rusted shrapnel.

It was Alex who first saw the shiny piece of metal on the ground, which he immediately picked up. Alexander mistook the odd piece of shiny metal to be the shard from a bullet. But his grandfather, Mr. Granhof, knew better. What

Alexander had actually recovered was an ancient 13th-century coin. A *Viking* coin!

Soon, Alexander and his grandfather started to uncover more coins . . . and then even *more* coins! When they were finally done searching, the team of grandfather and grandson had collected an amazing treasure trove of some 4,600 old silver coins! Many of the coins were Viking coins, minted in the Scandinavian region of the north (Sweden, Norway, and Denmark). Some of the coins proved to be English coins from the distant Middle Ages. Still others came from lands that now form modern day Germany and The Netherlands (Holland).

Alexander and Mr. Granhof notified authorities, who next day sent a team of archaeologists from their National Heritage Board to investigate. The archeologists, armed with metal detectors, retrieved an additional 2,400 coins, bringing the grand total to an amazing **7,000** long-lost and highly prized silver coins. The hoard's silver content *alone* was estimated to be worth **$265,000** — although collectors would pay far more for a chance to own these historic beauties. Many of the Lund coins are considered quite rare.

The forgotten stash, which for centuries had been buried in a pair of clay urns wrapped in cloth, was probably disturbed by a farmer who'd recently ploughed the field. The plow likely brought the coins to the surface.

"I never thought I'd experience anything like this!" exclaimed an excited Mats Anglert, one of the archaeologists tasked with recovering the rest of the coins. Mr. Anglert and the other elated archaeologists soon nicknamed the colossal find "Silverado."

"This is incredible," said a startled representative of the Lund University Historical Museum.

Scientists could only speculate why, many hundreds of years ago, someone hid such an enormous quantity of coins in the ground — and never returned to dig them up. The best theory offered is these coins were church taxes collected from farms and parishioners living in the surrounding Swedish countryside.

It was reported that young Alexander, who was initially somewhat awestruck and overwhelmed by his finding of such an immense treasure, quickly recovered to help archeologists with their dig. At last report, Swedish authorities had not yet determined the final reward for the Granhofs. We certainly hope their reward will be considerable.

Source: www.thelocal.se

Chapter 2 ♦ Jurassic Finds

Okay, so finding money is no doubt way cool. But did you know that some of the most spectacular archaeological finds in recent memory have been made by kids? We're talking dinosaur bones, dinosaur tracks, the horns of an extinct bison . . . and even the intact, frozen body of a long-dead woolly mammoth!

So, let's meet the kids who made these earth-shaking Jurassic finds. . . .

Seven-year Old Uncovers Extinct Bison Skull and Horns

On November 9th, 2005, young Joshua Bradford must have really been bummed when he learned he couldn't play video games. Joshua, 7, was supposed to spend the afternoon at an arcade in Sauk City, Wisconsin doing exactly that — playing high-tech games. Joshua had been paired with Mr. Bob Weiss, a local insurance agent, in the Kids Companion Program. Kids Companion, run by the Optimist Club, operates very much like the better known Big Brothers and Big Sisters Program. And so, on November 9th, Joshua and Mr. Weiss had agreed to meet at the local arcade.

Only problem was, seems the arcade was closed, and Mr. Weiss didn't immediately have a Plan B for how to spend the afternoon. Soon Joshua and Mr. Weiss found themselves driving around in Mr. Weiss' car, looking for something else fun to do. That's when Bob noticed how the water in the nearby Wisconsin River was running so unusually low.

In fact, the Wisconsin River was lower than Mr. Weiss, 63, had ever remembered seeing it. This also meant things usually underwater were now temporarily visible, making it an excellent opportunity for exploring.

So, Mr. Weiss opted for an afternoon scouring the water's edge, allowing Joshua to walk about thirty yards ahead, and Mr. Weiss to hang back some thirty yards behind. And while Joshua found numerous clam shells and other curiosities, Bob Weiss, a fisherman, busied himself with pocketing the occasional lost fishing lure that popped into view.

Suddenly, Joshua called out for his mentor to come take a look at something he had found. Whatever it was, it was sharp and pointy and poking up out of the sand.

"It looks like a piece of driftwood to me," shrugged Mr. Weiss.

"No, it's horns," said the boy.

Bob and Joshua began to dig, and soon freed the mystery object from the water's edge. And no doubt Joshua had just been proven right. The duo had uncovered a magnificent set of old horns with the animal's skull attached.

Mr. Weiss figured they had found the remains of an ox. Not a bad find, but nothing that unusual or extraordinary. With Joshua's help, Bob loaded the heavy, waterlogged, horned skull into the back of his car. Later, he brought Joshua's big find to Verlyn Mueller, the archivist at the Sauk-Prairie Area Historical Society. The archivist in turn consulted with Wisconsin State archaeologists John Broihahn and Steve Kuehn, who traveled to Sauk City for a first-hand look at the big skull.

Based on the size of the specimen, along with the unusual shape and curvature of the big horns, the archaeologists announced the find represented the remains of not an ox, but of a *bison*.

And not just <u>any</u> bison, but instead the Bison Occidentalis — a type of extinct bison that scientists say died off some 5,000 years ago. Only three had ever been found in Wisconsin (and none during the past 70 years), with Bob and Joshua's horned skull representing the largest Bison Occidentalis ever found in the state, and by far the eastern-most example of this species. Archaeologist John Broihahn called Joshua's bison "one of the best finds of the year, if not the best."

Joshua Bradford's bison turned him into something of a Sauk City celebrity. Joshua was asked to do newspaper interviews, appeared on local television, and was presented with a certificate of appreciation by the Wisconsin Historical Society.

Bob and Joshua have since turned over their skull to the Historical Society so that the unique skull and horns could be properly preserved and studied. At last report, archaeologists were planning to comb the banks of the Wisconsin River near Sauk City in hopes of finding more evidence of the rare Bison Occidentalis.

Treasure Kids!

Meanwhile, Bob and Joshua's discovery has been given a new name in Wisconsin. Folks are now calling it the "Bradford Bison."

Perhaps they should make that into a new type of video game. Maybe one with a catchy title, like "*Finding the Fossils.*"

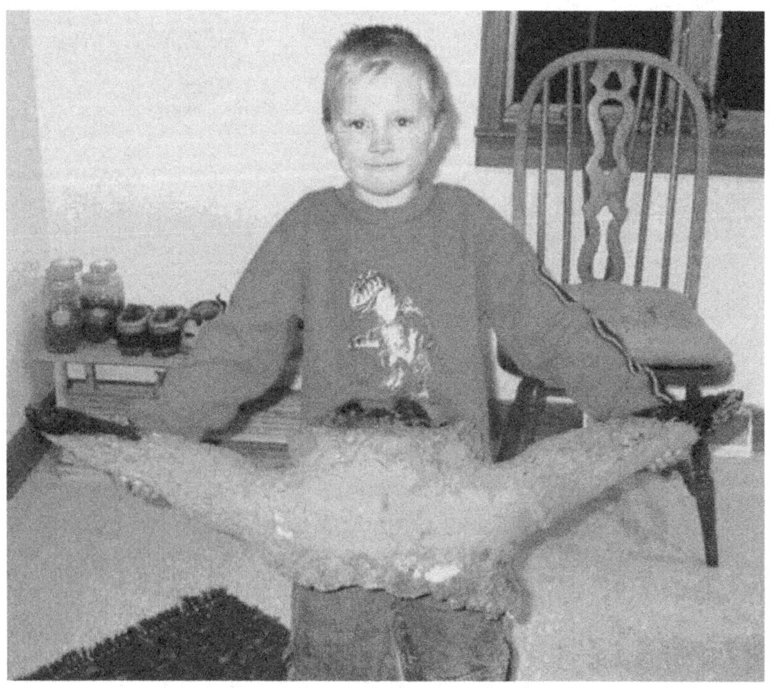

Source: *The Sauk Prairie Eagle*

Jurassic Prints Revealed in the Sand

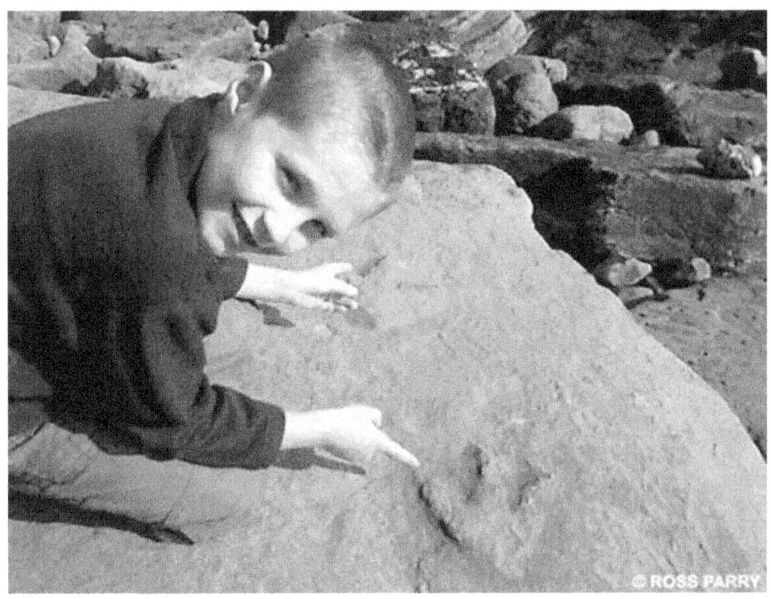

Source: www.dailymail.co.uk

An English boy walking along a beach with his father has found a perfect set of three-toed dinosaur footprints. Rhys Nichols, 8, of Scarborough, stumbled across this phenomenal pair of "trace fossils" in early 2008. Rhys often goes out beachcombing with his dad, Richard, as a way of finding fossils and other curiosities and collectibles. Rhys, who had been studying dinosaurs since he was three or four, is lovingly described by his mother as "dinosaur mad." "He must have every book going on them," she notes.

Scientists aren't sure, but their best guess is the prints are from a plant-eating lizard known as an iguanodon. The bi-pedal iguanodon (walked on two rear legs) lived during the early Cretaceous period, and perhaps as far back as the mid-Jurassic era. That means the animal which made the tracks Rhys discovered lived perhaps as much as 160 million years ago.

Said archaeologist Mr. Will Watts of the Scarborough Museums Trust, "This is a great find, as dinosaur prints are not normally that clear."

But these prints were so astonishingly clear and quite obvious, Rhys shouted out to his father, "Wow, Dad — look what I've found!"

Rhys' father, an area firefighter, immediately took photos of the three-toed tracks using his cell phone. This was a smart thing to do, as ancient "trace fossils" are easily disturbed and can be accidentally destroyed. The Yorkshire Coast where Rhys made his discovery has long been known for its abundance of fossil footprints. The general sandy, muddy conditions and sedimentary deposits there are excellent for making and preserving prints. It is thought that Rhys' iguanodon tracks were encased for millions of years high up in the sandstone cliffs that overlook North Yorkshire beaches. Occasionally, some of these rocks yield to erosion and come tumbling down onto the beaches below. Only this time, one of those big sandstone rocks contained the marvelously beautiful set of perfect dinosaur tracks that

Rhys so easily identified. As is typical with prints of this type, they were raised tracks instead of depressed, because wet sediment had filled up the original sunken tracks and then hardened.

Mr. Nichols mentioned that, because Rhys loves dinosaurs so much, he was "over the moon" at having found the footprints. "I couldn't get him away from them," explained Rhys' proud father.

Rhys' only complaint was that he wished the tracks were from a meat-eating dinosaur. The terrible Tyrannosaurus Rex is Rhys' clear sentimental favorite in the dinosaur realm.

Experts who've examined photos of Rhys next to the prints estimate the dinosaur that made them was approximately the same size as Rhys.

A decision was made to leave Rhys' tracks were they were found. Sadly, sometime later, it was discovered that the fossil prints had been removed by person or persons unknown. Luckily, the world still has the sharp, clear photographs of Rhys Nichols' snapshot in time — an instant from 160 million years in the past.

A Cat Named Thera

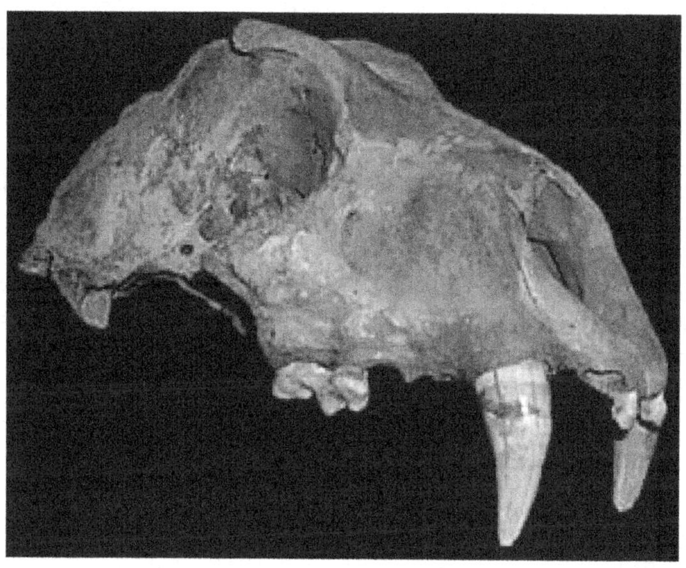

In the summer of 1995, a Wasilla, Alaska family took a canoe vacation north of the city of Fairbanks. Floating down a remote river in the state's ruggedly beautiful interior, the Fosters noticed how large chunks of the riverbank's permafrost had broken off and fallen into the water. Someone on the boat joked that wouldn't it be a blast if they were to discover a frozen saber-toothed tiger in the crumbling permafrost? Farther downstream, the Alaskans pulled ashore to relax for a time on a rocky beach. Twelve year old Devan Foster, the youngest member of the boating party, decided to use the time to go exploring on dry land. Devan had not wandered far when he happened to look under a bush and WOW — there it was. A large animal skull, just lying there by itself. Devan picked up the skull and brought it back to show the others.

Opinion was the skull, wonderfully intact except for the missing lower jaw, probably belonged to a deceased bear. But it had *mighty* large teeth for a bear, and something about the skull made it seem special, and somehow unique. The Fosters thought about maybe selling it to a tourist for a couple of hundred bucks. But that never happened, and so when they returned home to Wasilla, a suburb of Anchorage, the Fosters decided to take their unusual skull to the University of Alaska Museum, which is not far from downtown Anchorage.

When paleontologists and other scientists at the museum got a peek at Devan's find, it caused an immediate sensation at that institution.

No, Devan had *not* found a bear.

In fact, Devan had not even found the skull of a long-dead saber-toothed tiger.

What Devan had actually found was the *rarest* big-cat fossil find of all, the largest cat that ever walked the face of the Earth.

Devan had found Panthera Leo Atrox, sometimes referred to as Felis Atrox.

The fearsome head baring the nearly 5-inch long fangs belonged to the Ice Age lion, also known as the American lion. Extinct for the past 10,000 years, this deadly predator roamed from the steppes of Alaska and the Yukon all the way down through the lower 48 states and as far south as Peru in South America.

The boy quickly named the fossilized skull "Thera."

Standing five feet tall and at over 11 feet in length, the Ice Age lion weighed in at between 700 and 800 pounds. It hunted in small prides, feeding on wild horses and the steppe bison. Definitely at the top of the food chain, the American lion boasted a guesstimated bite force of 1,800 pounds per square inch — twice as powerful as today's

African lion. Unlike the modern lion, however, the males did not sport a mane.

Unfortunately, because Devan had found the skull on state land, the law (Alaska Historic Preservation Act) would not allow the youngster to keep his unusual prize. Warren Foster, Devan's dad, struck a deal with the University of Alaska Museum in Fairbanks, and also the South-central Alaska Museum of Natural History (now known simply as the Alaska Museum of Natural History) to donate Thera to these institutions. "Thera" would split her time between these two museums, one relatively close by the Fosters' home in Wasilla.

In an October, 1995 ceremony at Alaska's Museum of Natural History, Devan's friends, family, museum employees, and curious well-wishers watched as "Thera" the American lion was unveiled to the public. Devan was then awarded a certificate of appreciation for his donation of this amazing artifact to Alaska's museums.

It was also revealed that carbon-dating had placed Thera's age at 19,250 years!

Recently, in 2008, another American Lion skull, found by an unknown gold miner decades ago in an undisclosed location in Alaska's interior, went on the auction block in Los Angeles at Bonhams & Butterfields. The seller hoped to get as much as $45,000 for his Panthera Leo Atrox trophy. Bidding was reported to be in the tens of thousands of dollars, although the owner did not receive any bids close to his desired $45,000.

Meanwhile, paleontologist Roland Gangloff from the Fairbanks museum thinks Devan and his family did the right thing. "Be proud of the fact this fossil is where people can appreciate it," stated the scientist, who was on hand when Devan Foster received his award.

Thera is now the cat folks in Alaska like to visit, but no one would want to take home.

Dutch Boy's Memorable Day at the Beach

Source: Thomson Reuters

Jacob Walen, 10, was on vacation in sunny Portugal during the summer of 2003 when he made a most "extraordinary discovery" according to Portuguese paleontologist Octavio Mateus. While walking with his father on Paimogo Beach, not far from the coastal town of Lourinha, Jacob spotted what looked to him to be a curious piece of wood. Turns out the young schoolboy from the Netherlands had actually discovered not a piece of driftwood, but rather a piece of jawbone belonging to a ferocious flesh-eating dinosaur. This extinct predator lizard had walked the Earth some 150 million years ago.

The dinosaur, known as Torvosaurus (Greek for savage lizard), grew to a monstrous length of 35 feet and weighed in at around two tons (about the same poundage as a Mercedes Benz sedan or full-grown great white shark). The Torvosaurus was the largest known land predator of the Jurassic period, and preferred to lunch on baby sauropods with the help of its five-inch knife-sharp teeth. Sauropods were the giants among giants, the largest creatures that ever walked on land. Except for certain whales, the sauropods were the largest creatures that ever lived on this planet. And a hungry Torvosaurus was the sauropod's worst possible Freddy Krueger nightmare.

Actually, both Paimogo Beach and the town of Lourinha, which overlook the Atlantic Ocean from Portugal's western coast, have become famous for their numerous fossil finds. A wide variety of extinct species have been found in that region. Scientists at the Museum of Lourinha have reconstructed the menacing 4.6-foot skull of a Torvosaurus based on several finds from Western Portugal. Paimogo Beach is also the site of the largest nest of fossilized dinosaur eggs discovered anywhere on Earth. This amazing nest also boasted the only dinosaur egg specimens from Europe to actually contain dinosaur embryos. Fossilized dinosaur eggs are so rare that the first dino eggs weren't discovered until 1923 (in the Gobi Desert by the explorer Roy Chapman Andrews, the often-cited real-life inspiration for the movie character Indiana Jones). Up until 1923, scientists weren't even sure if baby dinosaurs were hatched or born live.

In 2008, five years after his discovery, a teenaged Jacob Walen returned to Lourinha to pose with his fossilized find in front of the museum's reconstructed Torvosaurus skull.

Dr. Mateus says that to find the skull bones of a meat-eating Torvosaurus is very rare, because the skull bones are thin and become separated from each other very easily. Luckily for young Jacob Walen, this fortunate treasure kid was in the just right place at the right time to make his awesome discovery.

Six-year Old Boy Discovers Bone from Winged Dinosaur

An amazing discovery was reported in 2007, the find being made by a six-year old boy! Owain Lewis, on vacation with his family at Great Britain's Isle of Wight, found bones from a 120-million year old flying dinosaur while walking on the beach at Compton Bay off the coast of southern England.

Owain and his father brought the spectacular find to the island's Sandown Museum, who then had the father and son present the bones to experts at London's Natural History Museum.

Paleontologists in London quickly agreed the bones belonged to a pterosaur, the long-extinct winged reptile from the Lower Cretaceous period (between 145 and 65 million years ago). At that time scientists say the Island of Wight was dominated by dinosaurs and gigantic, ferocious prehistoric crocodiles. Pterosaur (the "p" is silent and not pronounced) bones are especially rare because, like most flying creatures, the bones are lightweight and do not preserve easily. The adult pterosaur which left its wing bones for Owain Lewis to find would have had an imposing wingspan of 16 feet.

London paleontologists are not sure whether Owain's find represents the recently discovered Ornithocheirid pterosaur (the first such bones found on the Isle of Wight four years before Owain's discovery), or the more commonly known Istiodactylus pterosaur. Some 60 varieties of pterosaur are known to have existed, ranging in size from today's common sparrow (wingspan of just a few inches) to a monster with the truly incredible wingspan of forty feet (the size of many fighter planes!). That fearsome giant is known as Quetzalcoatlus.

Interestingly, pterosaurs did not flap their wings when they flew. Instead, they used powerful leg muscles to launch high into the air, and then opened their wings to glide.

Meanwhile, young Owain Lewis was reportedly very proud of his find, and especially about the fuss made over how important these reptile bones proved to be. Owain's mother and father are hoping that one day Owain will become a paleontologist. A *paleontologist* is the term for a scientist who studies the fossils of ancient creatures (both plant and animal) that no longer exist in today's world.

Russian Boy Makes Mammoth Discovery

Source: sites.Google.com

In 1997, a young Russian boy herding reindeer in the cold northern region of Siberia got the surprise of his young life. Nine-year old Simion Jarkov, a member of the Dolgan people, was roaming the frozen tundra near the home of relatives on Taimyr Peninsula, some 500 miles above the Arctic Circle. By chance, Simion stumbled upon a pair of huge curved ivory tusks poking out of the frozen ground. Scarcely believing his own eyes, Simion summoned his brother, Gennadi, for help in removing the tusks. Prized ivory from prehistoric beasts can bring in an enormous amount of money from collectors, and so members of the Jarkov family eventually transported the tusks to the village of Khatanga in an attempt to sell them.

French explorer and mammoth hunter Bernard Buigues learned of the beautiful tusks, and traveled to Khatanga to persuade young Simion and the rest of the Jarkov clan to lead him to the discovery site (on their reindeer sleigh!). The Jarkovs explained to the Frenchman that at least part of the prehistoric beast was still there, frozen in the ice. When Buigues dug down under the snow where Simion had found the tusks, he was astonished to find not just bones, but also flesh and hair frozen in time for some 20,000 years. Buigues could actually smell the enormous mammal! For the very first time, with the help of a nine-year old boy, a frozen Pleistocene specimen was able to be removed from the permafrost as a <u>complete</u> animal.

With assistance from The Discovery Channel, which agreed to pay for the cost of an expedition in exchange for film rights, scientists and engineers traveled to the remote Taimyr Peninsula to dig up Simion's mammoth. A huge 26-ton block was carved out of the permafrost using a portable generator and jackhammers. Then, with the help of the world's largest helicopter, the frozen mammoth was airlifted to Khatanga. There a team of international scientists, including famed Russian mammoth researcher Alexei Tikhonov, placed the frozen block of ice and mud in an ice cave for safe keeping. Since that time, scientists have been using Russian hairdryers to slowly thaw the beast, patiently studying small portions of hair, skin, organs, bone, and also prehistoric plants from inside the creature's belly. An enormous amount of new knowledge has been gleaned from young Simion's incredible discovery.

The Discovery Channel filmed its documentary, "*Raising the Mammoth*," based on the extensive research performed on this largely intact creature. Scientists believe this adult male woolly mammoth met his end when he became stuck in a large pool of mud and was, sadly, unable to extricate himself. The long-frozen muck helped to preserve the animal's enormous body for 20,000 years, until Simion came along at this desolate spot and saw the tips of the mammoth's tusks protruding from the ice.

Mammoths, ancestors of the modern-day elephant (and usually about the same size), lived from about four million years ago until just four thousand years ago. Now extinct, scientists have discovered an estimated 20 varieties of mammoth from the fossil record. These 20 varieties included a dwarf mammoth and also the better-known and larger cousin, the great *woolly* mammoth ("woolly" because of its shaggy hair — mammoths especially favored cold climates).

You can read all about Simion's discovery and how scientists excavated the creature in Woolly Mammoth, a book for kids written by author Windsor Chorlton.

And the name given to Simion's mammoth? It is known the world over as the *Jarkov Mammoth.* Talk about bragging rights! A nine-year old boy with a mammoth named after him.

Now that's way *cool* . . . even for someone in frozen northern Siberia!

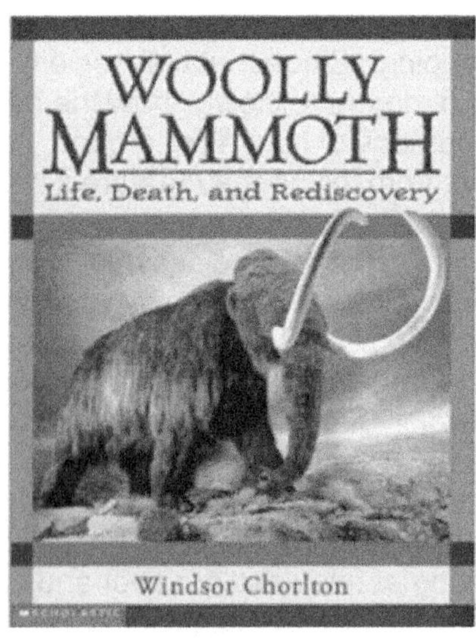

Chapter 3 ♦ Golden Boys

An old saying says that "there's no fever like gold fever." Over thousands of years, in every corner of the globe, the value of gold has been readily accepted by virtually all of the world's people. Gold hunters will stop at almost nothing to extract this precious metal from the Earth. People will do absolutely no doubt about it crazy things to find gold. Ever hear about the old "49ers" who travelled clear across the hazardous Old West to claim California gold, or the desperate people who braved the barren and frozen Yukon in 1898 for a chance to strike it rich on the legendary Klondike?

But some fortunate treasure kids — our own lucky "golden boys" — have managed to score it big by cashing in on the yellow metal. Here are their tales of incredible golden bonanzas. . . .

Tale of the Baltimore Treasure Trove

"Brother, can you spare a dime?"

Times were definitely tough in 1930s Depression-era America. Nearly 25% of the workforce was unemployed. One after another, banks and businesses closed their doors, often forever. Families lost their homes and farms. Long lines of weary, downtrodden folks stood outside soup kitchens, bellies aching for a hot meal. Others hustled selling apples or pencils on street corners, trying desperately to make ends meet.

"We have nothing to fear but fear itself," President Franklin Delano Roosevelt implored a distressed nation. But fear was everywhere — including fear's companions: poverty, hunger, homelessness, and hopelessness.

In 1934 Baltimore, two young neighborhood pals tried to pass the time by forming their own boy's club. Theodore Jones, 14, and Henry Grob, 15, called their newly founded organization the "Rinky Dinky Doos." After collecting petty dues from new members, Theodore and Henry decided to bury the dues, club papers, and assorted games (thought to be playing cards and dice) for safekeeping. The spot they chose was the hard-packed dirt floor in the cellar underneath the house where the Joneses rented an apartment. Both the Jones and Grob families (each fatherless) lived in a poor section of East Baltimore's harbor district.

After a few minutes of digging, Theodore Jones' shovel suddenly struck something unexpectedly hard. Theodore reached down and plucked a shiny disc of metal out of the ground.

"Hey look, a medal!" Theodore exclaimed.

But Henry Grob's eyes almost popped out of his head when he saw what his friend was *really* holding.

"You're crazy!" Henry laughed. "That's not a medal . . . that's a twenty-dollar gold piece!"

Sure enough, Henry was absolutely correct. In a flash, the boys were down on hands and knees, furiously digging in the hole. More gold coins began appearing. Then more coins. And then — even MORE GOLD!

Theodore and Henry began splitting the coins one by one. But soon they were finding so many gold pieces, these newly minted treasure kids began dividing their loot by the fistful!

After a while, as the hole got deeper, Theodore and Henry discovered two ancient copper gallon cans, the original containers for the thousands of coins.

Not knowing what to do with such an enormous treasure, the boys confided in Henry's brother-in-law, a fellow married to Henry's big sister. Because of all the bank failures and the financial panic sweeping America, President Roosevelt the year before had outlawed the ownership of gold coins (exceptions being made for older pieces owned by coin collectors). Henry's brother-in-law warned that the boys faced arrest if they tried to deposit the coins in a bank, or tried to exchange them for cash.

Henry and Theodore were advised to turn the gold over to the Baltimore Police, and so they did (or, at least, part of the gold!). Police promised the boys that if no one claimed the gold, the treasure would be theirs . . . although Theodore and Henry would have to take cash in exchange for the now forbidden gold coins.

The initial coins totaled $7,882 in face value — but when Henry and Theodore learned they would probably keep the treasure, they went back and brought in $3,562 more! Police could scarcely believe what they were seeing, two local teens lugging 3,558 gold coins to their station — in cigar boxes. That's $11,424 in face value, worth possibly *twice* that to collectors of the time. Today, with gold over $1,200 per ounce (it was barely more than $20 in the 1930s), those same coins would be worth *millions* and *millions* of dollars — especially considering no Baltimore gold hoard coin was minted after 1858.

The police turned the gold over to the courts. Newspapers in Baltimore and across America talked for weeks about the two poor boys who'd found the pot of gold. A Baltimore department store paid Theodore $3 a day just to stand in front of their establishment as a sort of "curiosity" advertisement. The boys were even interviewed on radio.

Meanwhile, every person who had any association with 132 South Eden Street (address where the pots of gold were found) went to court to claim the money. The elderly sisters who owned the apartment building claimed the money was theirs because the gold was found on their property. The family of a recently deceased jeweler claimed the gold belonged to them, because the jeweler had once lived in the building and was known to deal in gold. The heirs of a long-dead candle maker claimed the money his (and now theirs), because their family member owned the treasure house for 24 years beginning in the 1860s. The man was also known to keep large quantities of gold coins hidden at various spots in the house.

Long-time neighbors on South Eden Street told how the area was once home to many seafaring men, including several ship captains. Some of these sea captains were reportedly associated with the treasure house (previously one big house but recently divided into six apartments). Could one of these grizzled old captains be the source of all these gold coins?

In the end, the courts ruled in favor of the boys. They did so because none of the coins were minted after 1856. Since the copper pots had obviously been in the ground for fifty years or longer, no one who made a claim was successfully able to prove the treasure was theirs. The coins had probably been in the ground since the Civil War (1861-1865), some seventy years before their discovery, and the person or persons who buried them would, by 1935, be long gone.

In a May, 1935 auction at the Lord Baltimore Hotel, the now-famous Baltimore gold coin hoard brought in almost $20,000 in cold, hard cash. After lawyers' fees and expenses, each boy was set to receive nearly $6,000 for their 50% share of the treasure recovery.

Problem was, the courts decided to keep the boys' money until they turned 21.

Henry soon quit school and went to work in a mayonnaise factory packing jars for $16 a week. Theodore, who could barely read, had some scrapes with the law and wound up for a time in reform school. However, both lads seemed to have an awful lot of spending money for poor Depression kids — each boy owning not one but *two* cars.

Allegedly, the boys had later discovered a *second* stash of gold coins in the very same cellar. Sounds fishy? Well, many skeptics find this story hard to believe, especially since the famous cellar was so thoroughly searched by

Baltimore's finest, other apartment dwellers at 132 S. Eden Street, and also untold neighborhood folks who trespassed on the property. It is widely believed today that Theodore and Henry probably withheld many coins from the first discovery, and later explained them away by saying they were part of a much later discovery (highly unlikely).

What is definitely known is the boys' families had sold some undisclosed coins for cash to make ends meet. There were some "under-the-table" dealings directly with collectors and coin dealers who had approached the families.

In reality, the treasure had probably been much larger than the official tally of $11,424.

During a mysterious burglary of the Grob home (same East Baltimore neighborhood as S. Eden Street), someone supposedly made off with the lion's share of Theodore and Henry's so-called "second" stash of recovered gold coins. As they say, easy come, easy go.

In 1937, with Henry Grob only three years shy of collecting on his big 21st-birthday payout, Grob went swimming in the Baltimore Harbor and caught pneumonia. Henry died at South Baltimore General Hospital just days later. Mrs. Ruth Grob, Henry's mom, was eventually awarded the $5,798 that would have been paid to her son.

No one seems to know whatever happened to Henry's sidekick, Theodore Jones. His whereabouts are unknown — even to his own family.

The unbelievable discovery of the 3,558 gold coins beneath the dirt floor of a crumbling apartment house in 1934 Baltimore is the subject of a recent book. The book is Treasure in the Cellar: a Tale of Gold in Depression-Era Baltimore. In that book you can read who author Leonard Augsburger thinks is responsible for burying those coins in the basement, and why that person never returned to dig them up.

Gold Coins in Can Spark Montana Legal Feud

Way back in the year 1898, three boys roaming the hills just outside of Helena, Montana inadvertently caused a nasty legal ruckus that lasted for years. Horsing around, one of the boys decided to climb a tree while carrying an open pocketknife. Usually, this kind of reckless behavior involves a story about a hasty trip to a nearby emergency room. But, no, not this time. Instead, the boy accidentally dropped the blade, which fell straight down and struck the ground point-first, penetrating a few inches. The boys noticed an odd, metallic clink at the exact moment the knife-point struck dirt, and so decided to investigate.

Using the knife, the boys dug down to find, incredibly, a baking powder can filled with gold coins. The boy with the knife took all the gold home for himself. When the fathers of the other two boys learned what had happened, they demanded their sons receive a fair share of the bounty. The first boy refused, and was arrested for larceny. He was released from jail after a short while, and handed over the gold to authorities.

The authorities took inventory of the gold coins in the can, which amounted to about $1,000 — an enormous sum of money at time when a decent-paying job might bring in 25 or 30 cents an hour.

Angry about his arrest, the first young man and his family filed a lawsuit claiming libel . . . they said the arrest had unfairly tarnished the boy's reputation in the community.

The amount they sued for? Yep, you guessed it, *$1,000*.

Meanwhile, the gold coins were kept for safekeeping at the county clerk's office. No one was getting to keep or spend them while legal shenanigans were ongoing.

If all of this turmoil wasn't bad enough, next several area residents traveled to the county courthouse to put in their own claims on the gold. Each said that they had, *ahem*, buried the can filled with gold coins for safekeeping, and had expected to return later to retrieve their stash. Or, they'd buried the coins but had forgotten the exact location — and may thanks to boys for finding them!

Yeah, right.

The last the newspapers reported on this travesty, the county clerk was still in possession of the gold, and planned to dispose of the coins "through due process of law."

Certain treasures, it seems, are hexed. Not every treasure story has a happy ending. Treasure, surprisingly enough, does not always equal happiness.

There is an old Mexican curse that says, "May your life be filled with lawyers!"

Even worse, there's the dreaded Gypsy curse, "May you have a lawsuit in which you know you are in the right!"

We think surely some old Mexican or wandering Gypsy must have left those jinxed gold coins in the baking powder can under the tree just east of Helena, Montana. And they were very unhappy to learn those Montana boys had gone and dug them up!

Well, in the words of an old Arab curse, "May the fleas of a thousand camels lodge in his armpit!"

Brothers Discover Gold While Cleaning Henhouse

A couple of young Oregon farm boys discovered a treasure trove in gold coins in 1894 while cleaning out their neighbors' henhouse. W.O. Danielson, 10, and C.P. Danielson, 8, were being paid by a Mr. and Mrs. Roberts to clean out an old farm building on the couple's property. The unused, apparent henhouse hadn't been cleaned in years, and so the young boys set to work with their shovels, scooping trash into a waiting sled for later easy disposal. In court testimony ten years later, W.O. described how the brothers hauled piles of trash from the front of the hen house around to the back, and then began to shovel the refuse into the sled. But when the older boy's shovel struck something hard, the pair soon uncovered an old rusty half-gallon can in the pile of junk. The can was too heavy to lift with a shovel, and so W.O. tried prying off the rusted old lid with his fingers. W.O. figured the can was full of rocks, which needed to be dumped out. That would make the lighter and easier to lift. Taking a pick, W.O. then chopped through the can's lid, revealing a couple of old, musty tobacco sacks. But when the boys opened the sacks, they received an amazing surprise.

Treasure Kids!

It wasn't rocks making the old rusted tin can so very heavy.

It was stacks and stacks of gold coins.

The brothers collected the gleaming yellow coins and knocked on the door of the farmhouse. They told Mr. and Mrs. Roberts about finding the coins, and handed over the treasure when Mrs. Roberts told them, "Let's have it."

The Danielson boys then went back to cleaning out the hen house.

When they were finished the job, Mrs. Roberts paid the boys five cents for their efforts, and told them not to tell anyone about the gold. "We put the money there some time ago," explained Mary Roberts to the boys, "and were going to buy something with it. Don't say anything about it, and the Lord will bless you."

The boys then asked Mr. Dee Roberts how much was in the can. They were told "over *seven thousand dollars.*" That was an incredible fortune at a time when most workers only earned about $400 in an entire year — barely 22¢ per hour.

But the Danielson brothers did tell someone . . . they went home and told their family. The Danielsons then hired a lawyer and sued Mr. and Mrs. Roberts for their fair share of the treasure the boys had found.

In a landmark 1904 ruling, the Supreme Court of Oregon awarded the <u>entire</u> treasure of gold coins to the Danielson brothers. In doing so, the judges had reverted to an old English common law rule regarding "treasure troves." The judges found that since the old, rusted tin can obviously pre-dated the Roberts' ownership of the property (the gold was found in a 40-year old henhouse), and that several people had owned the land before the Roberts, the gold coins represented lost treasure. Buried treasure, according to the lawmakers, should be awarded to the lucky finders —

not to the landowners. "Owners of the soil acquire no title to a treasure trove by virtue of their ownership of the land."

By not offering to share the fabulous golden henhouse treasure with the deserving boys, the greedy Mr. and Mrs. Roberts had really laid one gigantic egg!

Teen Finds Huge Gold Nugget

Gold was discovered in California in 1848. A worker at Sutter's Mill in Coloma accidentally discovered a nugget from the American River lodged in a piece of the mill's equipment. The find set off the famous California Gold Rush of 1848-1855. The good news spread far and fast, and gold seekers the world over began pouring into California the following year. These fortune hunters would be forever known as "The Forty-Niners." It is estimated these Wild West miners would eventually pull a staggering 125 million ounces of yellow metal from the rich "placer" (free gold that often gets washed down river) and more deeply buried "lode" (or hard rock) deposits in the rivers and foothills of the Sierra Nevada Mountains.

But while most of the easy California gold has already long since been found, occasionally someone still gets lucky.

In 2008, 14-year old Jacob Hopkins became one of those fortunate people.

Jacob lives in the California town of Colfax, about 50 miles northeast of Sacramento. One summer day in 2008 the boy went fishing with his father, Mike Hopkins, and Jacob's older brother. While walking along the water's edge at Rollins Lake, not far from home, Jacob spotted something glowing in the water. Jacob waded in, reached down, and pulled out a potato-sized rock sprinkled with approximately six ounces of gleaming yellow gold.

Jacob stared at the rock in disbelief, thinking it couldn't possibly be gold. There was just way too much of it!

Mike Hopkins, an experienced gold hunter who often pans and sluices for gold, knew immediately that his son had made the find of a lifetime. At nearly $1,000 per ounce, the precious metal content of young Jacob's find was worth

$5,500 — and probably more to a collector of unusual rock specimens.

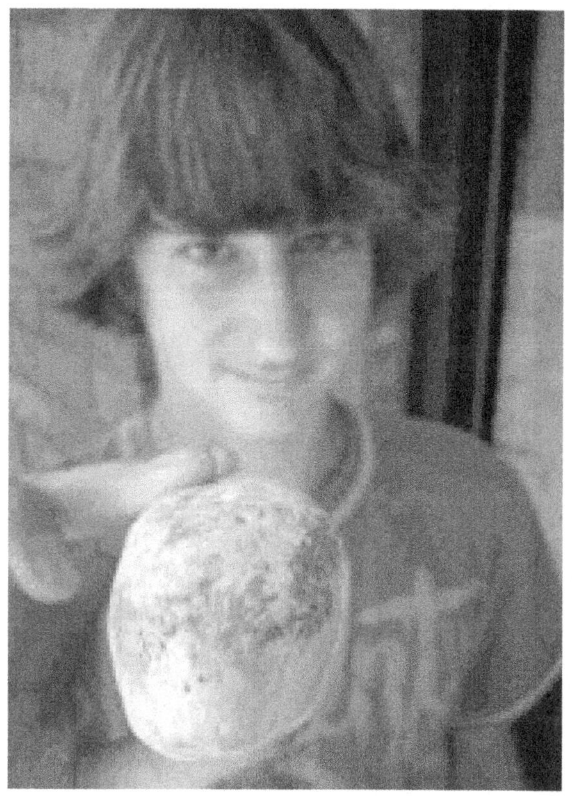

Spectacular finds seem to run in the Hopkins family. Back in 1982 while still in high school, Mike Jacobs found a four-ounce rock loaded with two ounces of gold. And on a recent trip to Alaska, Mike became the lucky discoverer of a small meteorite. But son Jacob's amazing find eclipsed even his father's very respectable recoveries.

After pocketing his golden bonanza, Jacob finished his memorable Saturday by reeling in a 15-pound catfish. Later,

Jacob decided to sell his prized find so that he could purchase a new trail motorcycle.

Meanwhile, news of Jacob's big score attracted droves of treasure-seekers to Rollins Lake. People with metal detectors and gold pans arrived to scour the area for more undiscovered gold. After all, while the Forty Niners dug up a staggering 125 million ounces, they didn't get *all* of the shiny yellow metal. Millions of more ounces lie buried in the Golden State.

Fourteen-year old Jacob Hopkins, out for nothing more than a leisurely trip to the local fishing hole, certainly proved that!

Iowa Boy Digging for Worms Finds Fortune in Gold

Way back in October, 1897, an Iowa boy digging for worms unearthed an absolute fortune in gold and other valuables. While searching for fishing bait on Beaver Island, which lies in the Mississippi River just south of Clinton, Iowa and directly across the Illinois state line, 16-year old Adolph Johnson made a most *incredible* discovery. Johnson's shovel struck something metallic, which soon proved to be a hastily buried iron box. Upon opening the box, the teenager was amazed to find some $50,000 in gold and paper money staring back at him.

The mystery of who buried the treasure box and why has never been explained. Obviously, no one ever stepped forward to claim this fortune in gold and currency.

One leading theory as to the gold's origin centers on a Swedish nobleman who had lived on Beaver Island for a number of years. The wealthy Swede had passed away just a few short years before Adolph Johnson's random discovery. Was this foreign nobleman the source of all this buried wealth?

The second, more intriguing theory involves the possible daring robbery of an express train. The world's first known robbery of a moving train occurred in Iowa, with the deed being committed by the notorious Jesse James and his band of desperate outlaws. The date was July 21, 1873 when the James/Younger Gang learned of a Rock Island Railroad train passing through Iowa that contained a $75,000 shipment of gold. The shipment was delayed, however, and the bandits were only able to carry away about $3,000 of the loot after successfully derailing the train. But with railroads in the 1800s routinely transporting cargoes containing millions of dollars in payrolls of gold, silver, coinage, and greenbacks, it was only a matter of time before moving trains replaced banks as the target of choice amongst criminals. After all, the robbers had the element of surprise when ambushing a train, and they had miles of empty track along which they could stop a train. Famous train robbers have included Bill Miner, Butch Cassidy, and of course, the legendary Jesse James.

Did 16-year old Adolph Johnson, digging for worms on Beaver Island, discover the hidden loot from one of the many Wild West's historic train heists? Unfortunately, we will probably never know. What is known is that author Mark Twain (Samuel Clemens) wrote many tales about fictitious characters such as Tom Sawyer and Huckleberry Finn involving themselves in high adventure along the banks of the mighty Mississippi River (including running away to an island on the Mississippi and even finding a box of gold). But young Adolph Johnson actually lived this type of adventure tale — for real — when he unearthed that mysterious box of gold and greenbacks on Beaver Island in 1897.

Treasure Kids!

Beep, Beep, Beep!

A young British boy out for his first metal detecting adventure made a truly spectacular find that will go down in history.

James Hyatt, only *three*, was finally getting to use his grandfather's metal detector in May, 2009. The device was nearly as tall as James. Having already shown an interest in the machine, James' father and grandfather agreed to take the boy to a local field in Essex, England. They could scarcely imagine what was about to happen next.

After showing James the basics, the youngster began to swing the search coil with encouragement from his dad and granddad. In less than five minutes, James got a signal that he had found something.

"It went beep, beep, beep," the boy explained.

Jason Hyatt, James' father, began to dig. At about eight inches below the surface, Mr. Hyatt saw a glint of gold. Carefully brushing away the soil, Mr. Hyatt lifted the mystery object out of the hole. When he saw the likeness of the Virgin Mary inscribed on a small square golden box, Mr. Hyatt thought at first someone was playing a trick on him.

But this was no trick — it was treasure.

Perhaps four million dollars' worth of treasure!

"We dug in the mud," a smiling James Hyatt would later say. "There was gold there. We didn't have a map . . . only pirates have treasure maps."

The Hyatts sought out expert opinion. What exactly had James found?

What James had uncovered, according to all experts who have examined the find, is a 500-year old religious pendant that once belonged to a powerful member of the church — or perhaps even the royal family of King Henry the 8th's day. The pendant is so rare that only three of its type are known to have survived from the 1500s. And those lockets have been valued — and sold — for millions of dollars.

Already, the British Museum and other well-known museums have expressed interest in James' find. That makes James not only a very lucky boy, but potentially a rich one as well.

The beautiful locket contains the image of Mary carrying Jesus' cross, and also the names of the three kings who followed the Star of Bethlehem to arrive at Jesus' birth in the manger. Those three Biblical kings were Caspar, Melchior, and Balthasar.

A government inquest officially declared the locket a treasure trove. Plans are for the relic to be sold to an interested institution such as the British Museum. The money would be split between the Hyatt family and the person who owns the field where the golden pendant was found.

The exact location of James' find in the town of Hockley has not been disclosed for fear of a swarm of treasure hunters descending on the location.

Experts have speculated the rare locket was lost in the field during a hunting trip.

Meanwhile, young James Hyatt has already found more than most metal detectors enthusiasts could ever hope to find in a lifetime. And he did it in just five minutes!

Anything more, as they say, would just be gravy. . . .

Chapter 4 ♦ Treasure Girls

If you've been paying close attention, you will have noticed that all of the young discoverers of treasure so far have been boys. Although boys have had an outstanding record over the years in finding treasure, the girls have certainly made their share of significant finds. And better yet, they seem to be catching up! No longer can it be said that boys rule when it comes to making amazing, unbelievable eye-popping discoveries.

So okay, girls — it's show time. Let's bring it on!

Girl Finds 2.93-Carat Diamond at "Finders Keepers" Park

In 2007, a recently graduated seventh-grader hit pay dirt during a family visit to the world's only public diamond mine, located in Arkansas. Nicole Ruhter, 13, had spent the entire June day digging and sifting with her parents, grandparents, brother, and two sisters. The family did not seem to be having any luck and, at 7 p.m., was preparing to call it quits.

So Nicole said a little prayer, desperately wishing to find something, no matter how small . . . *anything*! As Nicole and the Ruhter family headed down the service path from the digging field, suddenly Nicole saw what she later described as a "little shine" along the pathway. Reaching down, Nicole retrieved the shiny little stone and wrapped it safely in a dollar bill. Excited park employees later officially pronounced Nicole's find to be a gorgeous 2.93-carat tea-colored diamond. No one knows how many thousands of visitors must have walked right by Nicole's dazzling and valuable find. But they did!

The Crater of Diamonds State Park, just two miles outside of Murfreesboro, Arkansas, is a 37½- acre plowed field that sits atop one of the world's largest diamond-bearing volcanic pipes. The volcanic material exploded to the surface some 95 million years ago from miles beneath the earth's surface, spewing forth not only molten lava, but also diamonds, amethyst, agate, jasper, garnet, quartz, and calcite. In all, some 40 types of rocks and minerals can be found in what has been described as a "rock hound's dream."

The mine was discovered in 1906 when the pig farmer who owned the land spotted a peculiar shiny stone laying in some mud. Tests later proved the stone to be a brown diamond, and so the enterprising farmer soon transformed his farm into a mine.

In 1924, the largest diamond ever discovered in all the United States was unearthed in this Arkansas mine. Known as the Uncle Sam diamond, this white giant with a pink cast weighed in at a whopping 40.23 carats. The commercial operation also turned up spectacular prizes weighing in at 34.25 carats and 15.33 carats.

However, while the Arkansas diamond mine regularly produced gems of varying sizes, the subsequent owners of the property did not always turn a profit. Mining can be an expensive and frustrating proposition, and mines do not last forever.

In 1972, the State of Arkansas purchased the legendary old diamond mine, along with the surrounding 800+ acres of prime forest land. Over the past 38 years, visitors to The Crater of Diamonds State Park have been allowed, for a small fee, the privilege of roaming the property to dig and search for diamonds. It is estimated park visitors have found some 28,000 diamonds in that time, with the vast majority of those finds being under half a carat in weight (about the size of a match head or smaller). This is the only diamond mine on the planet that invites guests to search for precious minerals — and lets them keep what they find, no matter how big or how valuable! Park employees will even certify any diamonds you recover. In 1975, a man from Texas scooped up a 16.37-carat gem-quality white beauty now known as the Amarillo Starlight Diamond. On average, two diamonds are discovered on a typical day at Crater of Diamonds.

The park, not surprisingly, is a favorite place for kids, who have done quite well at finding treasure in the diamond field. As one observer notes, kids have very good eyes and are built closer to the ground, both great advantages when searching for that elusive bling in a pile of dirt and rocks. In 2006, eight year old twins were credited with discovering a 2.5-carat sparkler later displayed at a museum in Houston. Many years before that, it was reported a 14-month old baby left to wander the site was later found gumming an immense 11.92-carat dazzling white diamond. Talk about your beginner's luck!

There's no worry about the park running out of diamonds any time soon. Workers there routinely use tractors and bulldozers to expose fresh new unexplored ground. Visitors still report finding many hundreds of diamonds every year, with no letup in sight (and some never do report their finds to park officials, making the unofficial count undoubtedly somewhat higher).

As for Nicole Ruhter, 13, of Butler Missouri, she named her last-minute find *The Pathfinder Diamond.* At last report, Nicole was undecided whether to keep her storybook gem or sell it. While park officials generally refrain from placing a value on the finds of their guests, it is known that expert appraisals for a similar, slightly larger four-carat diamond found at the park ranged from $15,000 to as high as $60,000.

For information about Crater of Diamonds State Park, go to www.craterofdiamondsstatepark.com. If you visit the park, employees there will be happy to give you experienced tips on the best ways to hunt for diamonds. But if you listen to lucky treasure kid Nicole Ruhter, she'll tell you to make sure to say a little prayer!

Diamonds are definitely a girl's best friend. . . .

A Girl and Her Saber Tooth Cat

Being a junior ranger at Badlands National Park in South Dakota can be a lot of fun. Kids are supposed to learn about the park, spend a little time exploring, and come away with an appreciation of why Badlands National Park needs to be protected (it's got more than 64,000 acres of the U.S.A.'s largest prairie wilderness). At the end of their tour, kids hand in completed booklets and receive a Junior Ranger Day patch, pin, and certificate.

It is certainly not typical for junior rangers to make a major fossil discovery during their stay. And especially not the extremely rare skull and bones of the extinct saber tooth cat, one of America's most famous extinct animals.

This all happened on May 30th, 2010, when seven-year old Kylie Ferguson arrived at the park. Accompanied by family members, this was her very first time visiting Badlands. Kylie, from Sharpsburg, Georgia, had at least one huge advantage over most other junior rangers. Kylie's dad, Tom Ferguson, is a geologist, and so Kylie had learned some important things about fossils from her dad. Father and daughter had even done some fossil hunting together.

So, on May 30, while exploring behind the visitors' center, Kylie had some idea what she was looking at when she spotted some fossilized bones partially buried in rocky soil.

Kylie quickly summoned park rangers, who called in the paleontologists for their expert opinion.

Turns out the initial expert opinion was not correct. From the small portion of the skull and partial bones that were peeking out, scientists first announced that Kylie had discovered the remains of an extinct member of the sheep family. Not a bad find! But when heavy rains further exposed the bones just a few weeks later, giving fossil experts a better glimpse at the skull's teeth, there remained no doubt about what Kylie had found. Kylie, her mom, and her dad were in for a terrific surprise.

Source: National Park Service

The Fergusons got a call back home in Georgia informing them that Kylie had discovered the beautifully preserved remains of a saber tooth cat, an animal extinct for twenty million years. Intact skulls belonging to saber tooth cats, known by their scientific name Dinictis felina (Greek for "terrible cat"), are *exceedingly* rare. Usually, only small broken fragments are found. Fortunately, this particular cat's bones had been protected for millions of years by a deposit of limestone. That proved to be great luck for Kylie, the rangers, and the paleontologists who were most impressed with Kylie's find.

"All fossils are scientifically important," noted a spokesperson for Badlands National Park. "But this fossil is of *high importance.*" Kylie's saber tooth skull was being described by scientists as "museum quality."

According to Kylie, mom, Mrs. Jackie Ferguson, Kylie was really excited at the good news, and said Kylie's geologist dad will "just be over the moon" about his daughter's find.

Saber tooth cats of the Dinictis variety lived across the American Plains some 20 to 33 million years ago (during the Eocene and Oligocene "epochs"). A ferocious predator, these cats measured about 3½ to four feet in length and stood some two feet high, weighing in at a sleek 100 pounds — about the size of a very large dog. The saber tooth looked much like the modern leopard and would have lived and hunted in a manner similar to today's African leopard, except that Dinictis had flat feet and walked somewhat more like a bear than a cat.

At last report, technicians at Badlands National Park had carefully dug Kylie's fossil out of the limestone, and were preparing the cat's skull and bones for display. The Fergusons are planning a return visit to Badlands to see Kylie's saber tooth skull once it is ready for public viewing.

And Kylie? She couldn't wait for summer to be over so she could return to school and tell all her friends.

Couldn't wait for summer vacation to end? Couldn't wait to go back to school? Now *that's* excited!

Fifth-grader Finds Rare Dragonfly

As Kingsville, Texas fifth-grader Miranda Salinas stood in her family's garage, watching while her dad mowed the lawn, little did Miranda know she was about to make a most rare and unusual find. While her dad was busy mowing, Miranda happened to spot a dragonfly in the garage. Knowing her friend and classmate, Heidi Langschied, was a big fan of dragonflies, Miranda decided to capture the insect for Heidi.

"I held a box under it, and it climbed right in," said Miranda, speaking in a 2006 interview, the year in which she made the discovery.

Miranda gave the dragonfly to Heidi, who in turn brought the creature to her father, Tom Langschied. Mr. Langschied, a research scientist with the Wildlife Institute at Texas A&M University, could hardly believe what he was seeing when he peeked in the box. Ten-year old Miranda had captured a rare Amazon Darner dragonfly, a specimen almost *never* seen north of Mexico and the Rio Grande.

The rare dragonfly was kept for a time in Miranda and Heidi's classroom. The girls and their classmates soon named the dragonfly "Fred." Eventually, the fifth-graders voted to have the dragonfly preserved for study, and to have it donated to the university in Kingsville, at the research institute where Mr. Langschied worked as a scientist. Fred today is part of the Texas A&M's impressive collection of anthropoids.

The Amazon Darner dragonfly, typically found in tropical wetlands, had never before been spotted in Kleberg County, the county in which Miranda lives and where she discovered Fred. Miranda's find was particularly important because it indicated the creature's normal habitat may be expanding farther north into Texas.

"I was so surprised," said Miranda when she found out just how important her discovery had become, and what it meant to the scientists like Mr. Langschied who studied these insects as part of their work.

Dragonflies are easily recognized by their long bodies powered by double pairs of strong, transparent wings. They are the speedy, helicopter-like predators of the insect world, generally feeding on smaller insects such as mosquitoes, ants, bees, flies, and butterflies. They can propel themselves in six directions; upward, downward, forward, back, and side to side. The dragonfly is usually found near streams, ponds, lakes, and marshlands because their larvae (called "nymphs") need to live in water.

An Unexpected Treasure in Paradise

Aloha from the Big Isle of Hawaii! This next story is about a young girl, a Salvation Army thrift store, and an old Richard Simmons VHS workout tape. That's an unlikely combination for a treasure story, for sure, but treasure often turns up in some very strange places — and under the most unusual of circumstances.

In October 2008, an 11-year old Hawaiian girl named Mikela Mercier was visiting the Kona Salvation Thrift Store with her mother, Mrs. Jodi Mercier. Mrs. Mercier was in the store's dressing room trying on clothes, while Mikela waited in the main part of the store, checking out their selection of used video tapes. One video featured Richard Simmons, the frizzy-haired fitness guru who puts out all those fitness routines performed to music. Well, Mikela decided to take off the video's cardboard jacket to get a look at the cassette inside. And, that's when all the money came popping out. . . .

Ten $100 dollar bills, as in *$1,000!*

This puts a whole new meaning on that old Hawaiian surfer phrase, to "*Hang ten*!"

Mikela quickly summoned her mom from the thrift store dressing room. All those Ben Franklins were giving Mikela what Hawaiians call the "chicken skin."

That would be the same as goose bumps for the rest of us who don't live in the islands.

"Mom, we have to give it to the man," said Mikela.

"The man" would be Salvation Army Thrift Store manager Jimmy Thennes. Well, Mr. Thennes quickly put out a news release in an attempt to find the money's rightful owner, but that person never came forward. You see, many people hide money "for a rainy day" in some very quirky places, usually without telling anyone. Then if the person becomes ill or passes away, no one knows about their rainy day stash. That hidden cash can easily become lost, misplaced, or even thrown away. In 2007, a young mother of three children found $5,000 inside an envelope stuffed inside a pair of used pajamas at a Goodwill thrift store in South Carolina. Goodwill allowed the woman to keep the entire $5,000 — even though she was an employee at that store!

Sixth-grader Mikela, however, decided to donate her entire $1,000 find to the Salvation Army's Christmas Fund for needy people. Have you ever seen Salvation Army volunteers collecting money at Christmastime in those big red kettles? All of the money goes to charity to help the poor, the homeless, and people who don't have enough to eat.

"It is truly remarkable how a young girl like Mikela instinctively knew the right thing to do," said Mr. Thennes in an interview with the *Honolulu Star Bulletin* newspaper.

To Mikela, who was doing sixth grade in a Hawaiian language immersion school where classes are in Hawaiian (and even the kids' parents have to learn Hawaiian as part of the deal), we say "Mahalo nui loa, Mikela."

That's "Thank you very much, Mikela."

Treasure Kids!

We just hope Mr. Thennes didn't get *choke cars* outside the Kona Salvation Army store after folks learned about Mikela finding $1,000 in an old Richard Simmons tape.

"Choke cars" is Hawaiian slang for experiencing a traffic jam. Yes, it seems even in paradise they have traffic jams.

Aloha, treasure kids.

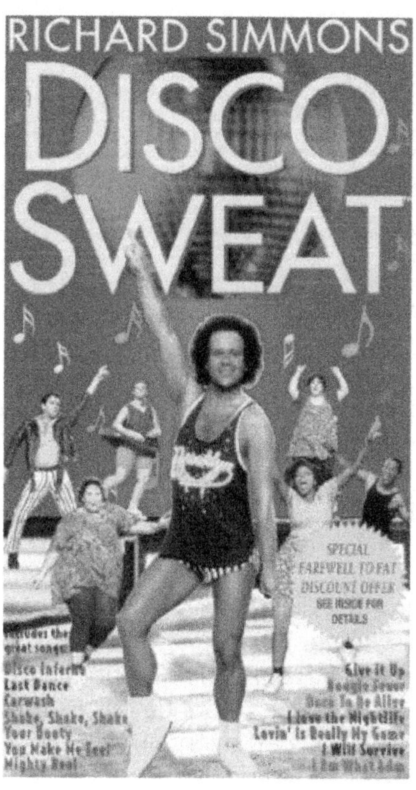

First-time Fossil Hunter Uncovers Ice Age Rhino

You don't have to be a famous paleontologist to find a rare fossil. In fact, you don't even have to be in the first grade yet!

In 2008, five-year old Emelia Fawbert of Gloucesterhire, England went with her father and grandfather on Emelia's very first fossil hunting expedition. The place they chose was a good one. Emelia, her dad, James Fawbert, and grandfather Geoff Fawbert, went hunting at the Cotswold Water Park in Gloucesterhire. Known as the "Jurassic Park" of Britain for its numerous fossil finds, Cotswold is the largest water park in the United Kingdom with 147 lakes spread over some 40 square miles. Most of these lakes were former gravel quarries that have since filled with water.

Treasure Kids!

Emelia's first fossil hunt, led by English paleontologists Neville Hollingsworth and Mark O'Dell, was attended by about 75 hopeful fossil hunters. Emelia, her father, and grandfather were just three of those excited searchers.

Emelia, who already owns a collection of toy dinosaurs and woolly mammoths, wants to be a paleontologist when she grows up. "I really like animals and dinosaurs," she tells her friends.

It was Emelia whose sharp eyes first spotted the fossilized bone sticking out of the clay at the recently excavated gravel pit. Emelia called for her dad and granddad to help. Using a trowel, Emelia and her father carefully dug out the 16-inch oddly shaped fossil bone.

"To be honest," admitted Emelia's grandfather, "none of us really knew what it was."

But to paleontologists Neville Hollingsworth and Mark O'Dell, and other experts who have since examined Emelia's find, there is little doubt about what the five-year old amateur fossil hunter had found. Emelia had found the atlas vertebra of a nearly 50,000 year-old woolly rhinoceros. In life, this particular vertebra was located in the animal's neck, and helped to support its massive head.

"It was spectacularly rare to find something like that, and even more incredible for someone so young to find it," commented Dr. Hollingsworth. The British paleontologist himself has been credited with some major finds, including the remains of another woolly rhinoceros in nearby Swindon, as well as the skull of a woolly mammoth.

The woolly rhinoceros species, once a native of both Ice Age Europe and Asia, is thought to have lived between 20,000 and 50,000 years ago. A plant-eater, the huge beast had long, shaggy, gray-brown hair plus two thick horns made out of matted hair. We know something about this animal's appearance because it was featured in cave paintings made by early humans. The cave people hunted the woolly rhinoceros for its meat.

To Amelia's surprise, she was allowed to take home her fossil find. However, Emelia and her family later decided to have the woolly rhino's vertebra preserved in a special substance, which was applied by Dr. Hollingsworth. Emelia's family planned to donate the specimen to a museum so many more people could appreciate Emelia's fossil and learn about it.

No other parts of Emelia's woolly rhinoceros have been discovered at Cotswold Water Park. The ancient River Thames may have, countless years ago, carried the rest of the rhino's remains off towards London. That is according to park education officer Ms. Jill Bewley.

"It was a fantastic find for Emelia and her father," added Cotswold's Ms. Bewley. "These experienced guys spend hours and hours in the quarry, and along comes sweet little Emelia and makes the find of her life."

For her part, Emelia has been busy studying about her new favorite extinct animal, the fearsome woolly rhino. "When it was alive it would have been really big with a lump on its back, a big horn, and very furry."

". . . . I always wanted to be a paleontologist," Emelia was sure to add.

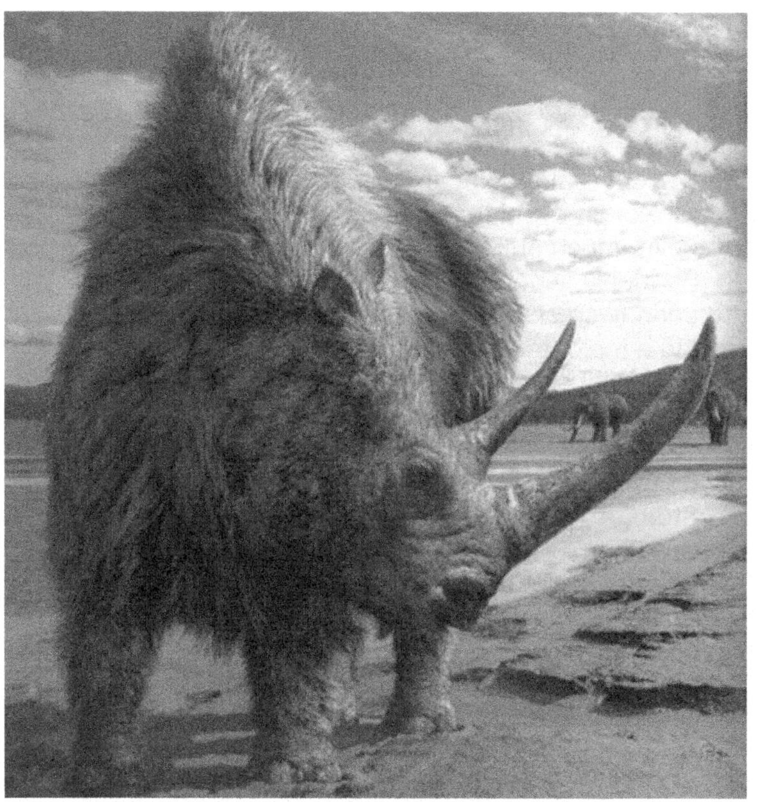

Source: extinctionaroundtheworld.blogspot.com

Treasure Kids!

Money from Heaven!

On Friday evening, October 9th, 1992, treasure struck the town of Peekskill, New York. Michelle Knapp, 17, was hanging out with a friend in her Peekskill home, entirely unaware of an event that was quickly unfolding across the skies over much of the northeastern United States.

Suddenly, just before midnight, there came a tremendous crash from directly in front of the Knapp home. Fearing a major traffic accident had just occurred on her normally quiet suburban street, Michelle rushed outside to see . . . *nothing*. No smashed cars. No broken glass. No injured drivers.

Seemingly nothing out of the ordinary.

Strange.

But when Michelle turned to reenter her home, she caught sight of her red 1980 Chevy Malibu parked in the driveway. A typical first car, it was an old clunker Michelle had purchased from her grandmother for $100.

Michelle was horrified to see that someone, or something, had smashed in the rear passenger portion of her car, completely crunching the corner of the car's trunk and taillight in the process.

A large, suspicious rock was spotted lying on the ground underneath the trunk. Michelle dialed 911. That Peekskill cops arrived, smelled a gasoline leak, and promptly called the fire department.

To everyone's surprise, when the hefty 27-pound rock was pulled from underneath the Malibu, authorities observed what appeared to be a small crater blasted out of the driveway concrete.

No ordinary vandal had caused this damage. Laboratory tests performed on the suspect rock, when coupled with news reports coming in that evening from West Virginia to Pennsylvania, eventually solved the mystery of Michelle Knapp's "vandal."

What had smashed Michelle's Malibu into barely recognizable junk was a 27.3 pound (12.4 kilogram) rock from space. A stony, chrondite meteorite which had been hot-roding around the solar system for millions of years.

Lucky for Michelle and her guest, the falling, smoldering rock had missed the Malibu's gas tank by just inches. But the teen's Chevy was, nonetheless, a complete loss, looking like it had been hit by a bowling ball thrown from a passing jetliner.

First seen in the skies over Kentucky, the meteor had streaked towards the Northeast, passing over West Virginia and then Pennsylvania in a matter of 30-40 seconds. Folks at Friday night high school football games videotaped the brilliant fireball for posterity. In all, some 16 videos were made of this now famous meteor turned meteorite.

From an analysis of the videos, meteorite experts have concluded that the "Peekskill Meteor" exploded into as many as 70 separate fragments. But only one of those fragments was ever discovered.

That would be the 27-pound fragment that crunched Michelle Knapp's car.

Because it was witnessed by thousands on a cool autumn night, and caught on numerous video cameras, the Peekskill Meteor became one of the most famous American fireballs in history. Just go to YouTube.com and type in "Peekskill Meteor" to view samples of the many videos of this amazing visitor from space as it lights up the night sky.

And 17-year old Michelle Knapp of Peekskill, NY? Whatever happened to Michelle and her poor Malibu?

Not to worry. Michelle put her famous space rock up for auction, and received in the neighborhood of a cool $75,000 for her trouble.

And the red 1980 Malibu? Junked, might you ask?

No, not junked. Sold to R. A. Langheinrich Meteorites for the amazing sum of $25,000!

Michelle Knapp, becoming an official treasure kid, went out and bought herself a brand new car with the money that fell from the sky.

The 1980 Malibu has since traveled the world, attending mineral and meteorite shows from Japan to France to Switzerland to Germany and back to the good ole USA. People always flock to see "the car that was crunched by a meteorite."

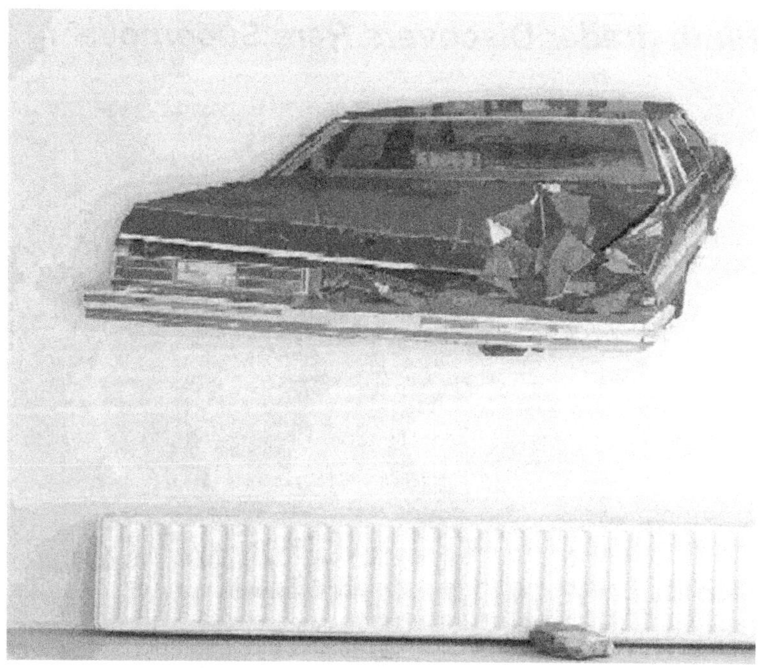

Source: R. A. Langheinrich Meteorites

Ninth-grader Discovers Rare Supernova

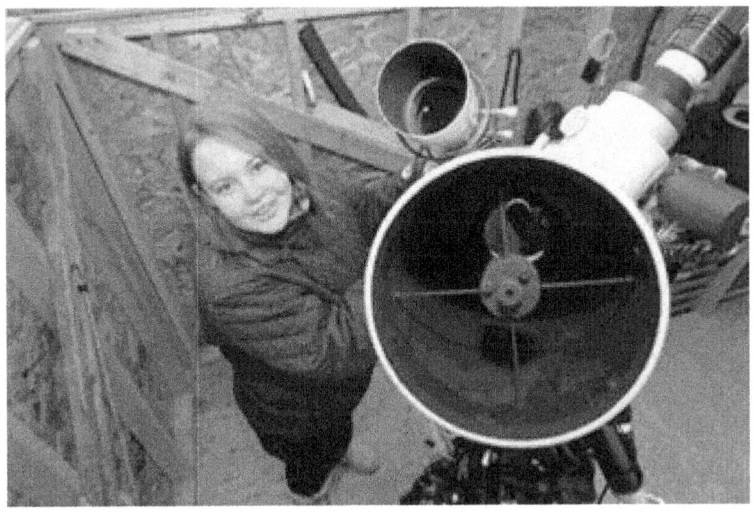

In November, 2008 a 14-year old girl became the youngest person on record to find and identify a supernova. Caroline Moore from Warwick in upstate New York, a budding astronomer with ten telescopes in her growing backyard observatory, was also credited with discovering one of the most unusual and rarest types of supernova ever spotted.

A supernova is the explosive death of a star, with the dying star having reached the end of its long lifecycle after burning brightly for billions of years. The heat and light given off by such a celestial event is indescribably enormous. Supernovae become many *millions* of times brighter than even our own sun.

Interestingly, Caroline did not discover this supernova using one of her own telescopes. Rather, as a member of a "supernova" team of 28 amateur astronomers from five countries who regularly look for tiny changes in space,

Caroline found the odd, undiscovered supernova by closely inspecting someone else's photos from space. These deep space images were taken by Mr. Jack Newton on a 16-inch telescope in Portal, Arizona. But it was definitely Caroline who deserves credit for using the images to spot something no one expected to see.

Caroline's discovery, known to astronomers as SN 2008ha, is so unusual because it is so very unexpectedly weak. In fact, that may explain why no one else saw SN 2008ha before Caroline. You see, there are *supernovae,* unbelievably massive nuclear explosions that rip and tear apart a dying star from inside. And then there are regular novas, smaller (though still titanic) explosions which erupt from the surfaces of unstable stars. Yet Caroline's find, while being *1000* times brighter than a *regular* nova, is still *1000 times less bright* than the typically gargantuan *supernova*.

Astronomers are hailing Caroline's supernova as a rare new type of <u>hybrid</u> supernova (somewhat of a cross between a regular and supernova). Giant telescopes in observatories from Chile to Hawaii to Arizona have since been training their colossal lenses at SN 2008ha, which is located in a very distant galaxy (called UGC 12682) some 74 million light years from Earth. Even one of NASA's orbiting satellites has been used to get a better look at this peculiar oddity, which has scientists speculating and debating as to its cause.

There are two interesting leading theories on SN 2008ha. One theory is that this "wimpy" supernova is really a massive supernova that has collapsed upon itself, forming a powerful black hole (with the suction-like black hole only letting escape a tiny fraction of the explosion's light and energy). And the other contending explanation is that SN 2008ha is a failed supernova — a partial, interrupted explosion that for some unexplained reason did not destroy the entire star (as supernovae almost always do).

Meanwhile, the now-famous Caroline Moore continued to attend Warwick High School in New York, living the life of an otherwise normal teen. She much enjoys singing, as well as being a member of the Warwick High School ski team. Caroline's proud father, Mr. Robert Moore, for years a big booster of his daughter's pursuit of astronomy, has recently reported that Caroline has also discovered boys.

It is not known if Caroline will eventually become a full-time professional astronomer, or if she will simply continue to pursue stargazing as a passionate hobby. Regardless of her choice, like a meteor streaking across the night sky, 14-year old Caroline Moore has already left her dazzling mark on the learned and seemingly mysterious world of astrophysics.

Mr. Alex Fillipenko, the leader of the University of California at Berkley's supernova group, had some very interesting praise for Caroline's incredibly important work. "This shows that no matter what your age, anyone can make a significant contribution to the understanding of our Universe."

Young people may have the greatest gift of all when it comes to making potential discoveries . . . the gift of time.

Time is on your side, treasure kids . . . but only if you decide to make use of it.

Chapter 5 ♦ Amazing Adventures

Sometimes kids go looking for a little adventure . . . and find more thrills than they ever bargained for! Here are some unusual stories about treasure kids who went in search of a bit of excitement — only to wind up making headline news by uncovering some things totally unexpected. Sit back and prepare to be amazed. . . .

Before Indiana Jones. . . .

In 1928, London schoolboy Gerald Grimsdell dreamed of becoming a famous explorer. He wanted badly to follow in the footsteps of famous men such as Leif Ericson, Marco Polo, Christopher Columbus, Juan Ponce de Leon, and Britain's own Henry Hudson. Gerald admired these famous individuals who had sailed the world, faced danger, and made fantastic discoveries.

Home from school one day on holiday, the bored nine-year old decided that, as a budding explorer, he should go in search of buried treasure. Excited, young Gerald grabbed a shovel and headed for the garden in the backyard — and began digging. Gerald must've had a good breakfast that day, because he dug a hole almost four feet deep.

Suddenly, Gerald's spade struck something hard. Brushing the dirt away, the boy could see what appeared to be an old earthenware pot. Then, the unmistakable gleam of silver began to peek out. Coins! Hundreds and hundreds of valuable ancient coins began to show themselves to Gerald, almost as if by magic. The boy quickly went to summon his stepfather.

Gerald's stepfather happened to be Major George Cyril Carpenter of the British Royal Artillery. Major Carpenter promptly notified London authorities of Gerald's discovery, and the treasure was immediately taken into custody. An inquest was held, which quickly determined that young Grimsdell's cache of coins amounted to a treasure trove. The earthenware pot was found to contain some *652* silver Roman coins approximately 1,800 years old. This surely was a "treasure trove" by anyone's standards, and certainly one of immense proportions.

Under British law, a jury of citizens was given the task of deciding the ultimate fate of Gerald's treasure. Again, following existing law, the jury determined the 652 coins were the rightful property of the British Crown (government), with the coins to be turned over to the British Treasury. However, it was also determined that, as the discoverer of the treasure, Gerald Grimsdell was entitled to a full 80% of the estimated value of the Roman silver. This reward was to be based on an estimate of what the coins would bring if sold to the public. In the end, Gerald and his family received a fortune in finder's fees for his highly improbable stroke of good luck.

London, originally known by its Latin name Londinium, was founded by the Romans after their invasion of 43 A.D.

A large part of what is today Great Britain would become a Roman outpost in the North Atlantic. Londinium was built where the River Thames was narrow enough to build a bridge, but deep enough for the Romans' ocean-going ships. Although Londinium originally served as a civilian settlement for the purpose of trade and commerce, there is evidence that it also served as a fortress — and home to the famous Roman Legion. We will probably never know who buried that earthenware pot with the 652 coins — or why. Best guess was it was a Roman official or merchant. And mystery of why that person never returned for the treasure also has no easy answers.

What is known is that after Gerald Grimsdell's much-heralded find, Major Carpenter searched the grounds of his home and was successful in recovering even more Roman silver.

Meanwhile, Gerald Grimsdell became the envy of nearly every child in Great Britain, being the celebrated boy who had searched for buried treasure — and actually found it!

Kids with Metal Detector Make Unexpected Find

The Andraka family kids of Maryland just wanted a fun birthday present, something big, something a little different. So in 2006, Mr. and Mrs. Andraka decided to pool birthday money for all three of their kids . . . Nicole — age 7, Zack — age 5, and baby brother Sean — just 2. That meant *all* the Andraka kids would be getting one present to share . . . but it would be one *big* present. . . .

Something having to do with science. . . .

Well, it turns out the kids' parents went to Radio Shack and bought them a metal detector.

Uh oh, Spaghetti-Os.

The Andraka kids immediately took the metal detector in the woods behind their home near Owings, Maryland.

Meanwhile, the kids' mom worked out back in the family garden, where she could keep an eye on what the kids were doing.

Not long afterwards, the kids came back to her carrying a piece of metal. And then another. And then, yet another piece of metal. Hmmm. . . .

Mr. and Mrs. Andraka figured someone must be using the woods to dump pieces of junk.

But next, Nicole, Zack, and Sean came home with an odd piece of metal with *rivets*. Years before, when Mr. and Mrs. Andraka had first bought the land and began to build the family's new home, a neighbor had mentioned to them how the place had a history. Used to be the site of a farm owned by a Mr. George Scaggs. . . .

And that a plane crashed on the farm many years ago.

A *plane*? Planes are put together using thousands of rivets, which are bolts of metal used to fasten together pieces of metal.

Then the kids came home with pieces from the aluminum skin of an airplane. And wires. And even pieces that looked like parts from a cockpit seat.

Now there was little doubt about it. The Andraka kids had found remnants left over from the 1955 crash of a military jet. This particular jet was a Lockheed T-33a "Shooting Star" training model (much like the one in the photo), used to help new pilots practice their skills.

On September 3, 1955, the jet took off from a base in the state of Wisconsin, headed for Andrews Air Force Base just outside of Washington, D.C. — and only a few short miles away from the old Scaggs Farm. As the twin-seat T-33a, nicknamed by pilots the "T-Bird," neared Andrews Air Force Base, the pilot started to realize the plane's electrical system was not working properly. Knowing it was too dangerous to try to land the malfunctioning plane at an air base, the pilot flew the T-33a out over the countryside, looking for a place to "ditch." While radioing a "mayday" distress signal to the base, the Air Force pilot looked down and spotted a farm next to a big patch of woods. Careful to not hurt anyone on the ground, the pilot aimed his plane directly towards those secluded woods. With his cockpit now on fire and filling up with flames and smoke, the pilot hit the "eject" button and was shot up and away from the plane. An emergency parachute carried him through the sky and away from danger. The burning T-33a screamed down into the woods where it crashed with a tremendous noise, destroying the jet upon impact. The pilot was lucky enough to float down into a tree where his parachute got caught up in the branches.

The Air Force quickly sent a helicopter to the site to rescue the pilot from the tree. They also sent accident investigators, emergency crews, and cleanup specialists to the old Scaggs Farm to deal with the awful mess the crash had caused.

They recovered most of the plane — but obviously not every bit of it.

Years later, Mr. Scaggs sold his farm. More years went by, and people moved there and built houses. Eventually, the Andraka family moved in too, last house on the street with their property right by those woods.

Yes, the very same woods where the jet called the "Shooting Star" had crashed a half century before.

For some two years, the Andraka kids would team up using their metal detector, collecting a very interesting pile of parts from that long-forgotten plane. Nicole would swing the detector, listening for the beep that said they'd found metal. And brothers Zack and Sean would dig up what Nicole had found.

Nobody knows if the pilot of the "T-Bird" is still alive. If so, he'd be an old-timer by now, well past retirement age. But the Andraka kids would like to meet him if possible, to show the pilot what they've found from his old jet. And also to ask him in his own words what it was like the time he ditched his T-33a in the woods on the old Scaggs Farm, the same woods that now sit directly behind their backyard.

Meanwhile, late-breaking news about the Andraka kids is they've taken up a brand new hobby related to science. They are now building and setting off rockets as members of a local model rocket club.

And Mrs. Andraka? She has since written to the folks at Andrews Air Force Base, asking them for more information about the unnamed pilot and his T-33a Lockheed jet, serial number 53-5261, which came down unexpectedly on the Scaggs Farm that fateful day in September, 1955.

We just ask the Andraka kids to remember one very important, very simple rule when firing off those model rockets:

What goes up, must come down.

History in a Bottle

When buddies Adam Giles and Derek Hann went digging in their backyards in 2008, little did the boys know they were about to discover an important piece of American history. Derek, 12, made the first find, a bottle lying about two feet underground. This unusual bottle, with letters that spelled "**FRASER**," seemed interesting to Adam and Derek. It did not look anything like bottles the boys were used to seeing in supermarkets near their suburban Fairfax County, Virginia homes. In fact, the **FRASER** bottle sported what glass experts call a "pontil scar." This type of scar is the telltale mark of a hand-blown bottle. Hand-blown bottles are unlike modern bottles, which are machine made in today's glass factories. When Adam, 13, next found the remains of yet another old bottle and some unidentified brown glass shards — not like any glass the boys had previously seen —

the two young friends decided to find out more by using the Internet. This proved to be a very smart move. The boys eventually brought their questions about the bottles to Ms. Aimee Wells, an employee at Fairfax County's Cultural Resources office. Ms. Wells holds a college degree in anthropology from nearby George Mason University, and has done much research into the history of the Chesapeake Bay region (Fairfax County is a suburb of Washington D.C. and lies just west of the Chesapeake and the United States capital). Ms. Wells let Adam and Derek know about a computer program that can electronically place old maps on top of modern satellite photos of the Earth. Google Maps is one such program that you or anyone can use on a home computer to see photos taken by satellites in space — aerial photos of your house, street, neighborhood, town . . . just about anywhere.

What Adam and Derek soon learned was amazing. The computer program took an old Fairfax County map and placed over a satellite photo of the boys' neighborhood. When it did so, it immediately told the boys their backyards had once been part of a huge military encampment called Camp Alger. The year was 1898, and the United States was at war with Spain in a conflict the history books call the Spanish-American War. The former Camp Alger covered some 14,000 acres (more than 20 square miles) across what are today the towns of Falls Church and Vienna. Adam and Derek's backyards were likely the location where soldiers from an Ohio regiment lived in temporary tents. There they huddled and waited for orders to ship out and join the front lines (action was seen mainly in Cuba, Puerto Rico, and the Philippines). Today, nothing is left of Camp Alger — except for buried artifacts — and some old military records still on file. Those records show how soldiers from Camp Alger played baseball and musical instruments to pass the time. The records also describe how the men were forced to march seven miles to the east every week — to the banks of the Potomac River — just to take a bath!

A long-gone American soldier probably once held that **FRASER** bottle in his hands while awaiting orders.

Camp Alger was eventually closed because of an outbreak of the deadly typhoid fever. Still, the United States defeated Spain in the four-month war, effectively ending Spain's long reign as a global colonial empire.

Adam and Derek's backyards have since been added to the list of important archeological sites in Fairfax County, Virginia. The boys were given further instruction on how to dig safely, using basic archeological techniques. Adam and Derek were also shown the proper way to log what artifacts they found (and where), so that anything the boys might find could be shared with archeologists and historians doing similar work.

Ms. Aimee Wells has since been promoted to staff archeologist for Fairfax County, and is working on her master's degree from the University of Leicester.

Treasure Kids!

When it comes to bottles, treasure kids Adam Giles and Derek Hann are far from alone. Many avid relic collectors and treasure hunters focus their interests *specifically* on finding ancient bottles. Certain old bottles are highly prized and can be extremely valuable, for trade or for sale. Also, field archeologists routinely use ancient bottles and bottle fragments as important clues to a site's history, and are careful to identify and date specimens they uncover at their dig sites.

Remember that old saying, "One man's trash is another man's treasure!"

And to collectors, bottle hunters, and archeologists, 110-year old bottles such as the beauties discovered by Adam and Derek are most definitely treasure. . . .

Treasure Kids!

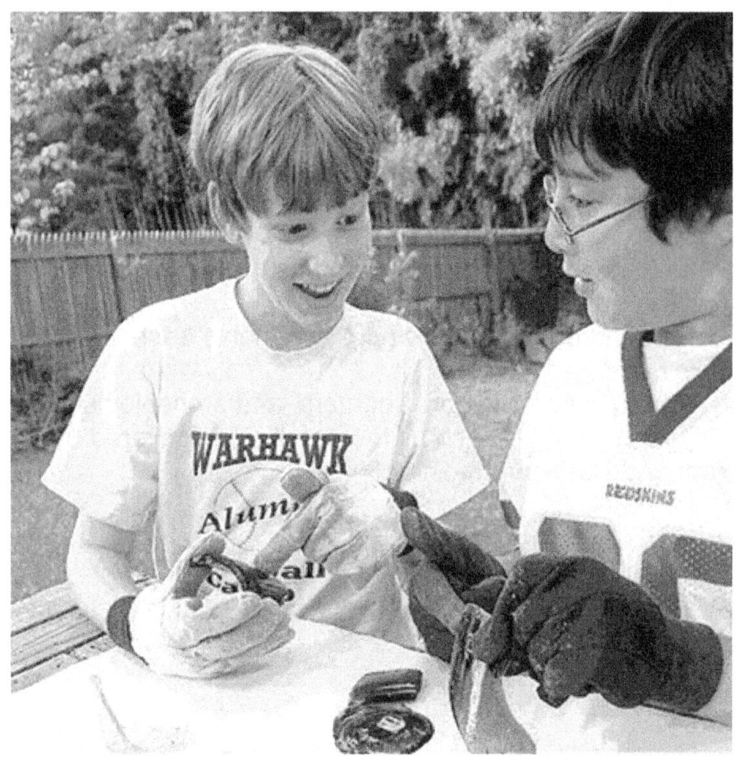

Source: *The Washington Post*

Ten-year Old Helps Solve Crime, Collects Reward

Source: www.cielodrive.com

In December, 1969 when 10-year old Steven Weiss found an unusual-looking .22-caliber revolver on the hillside behind his Los Angeles home, he knew exactly what to do. Steven watched television police shows and was therefore very careful to pick up the gun by its barrel. Steven did not want to touch the handle or trigger area, which might contain fingerprints. The boy immediately brought the handgun to his father, who in turn called Los Angeles Police. To Steven's horror, the policeman who came to the Weiss' home was not so careful about handling the mysterious handgun. The policeman did not seem to think Steven's discovery was all that important.

During the summer of 1969, one of the most horrible crimes in United States history was committed in Los Angeles, in a neighborhood not far from Steven's home. A beautiful and famous Hollywood actress, Sharon Tate, was murdered at her rented Beverly Hills mansion along with several of her houseguests. Police were at a loss to explain who would want to hurt the people at Ms. Tate's house, and why. And so for many months the killers remained free as police desperately searched for clues to solve the case.

When Bernard Weiss, Steven's father, later learned the killers had used a .22-caliber handgun during the commission of their crimes, he called the police station to find out whether the gun Steven had found had been tested. In fact, Mr. Weiss had to make many calls to police, who seemed to be ignoring both him and the gun Steven had discovered. Meanwhile, during this time, the unusual antique "Buntline special" revolver sat forgotten and untested in a Los Angeles Police evidence locker. One policeman Mr. Weiss spoke with told him that thousands of guns were turned in to the Los Angeles Police every year, and that L.A. Police collected so many guns that they were eventually "thrown into the ocean."

Frantic that crucial evidence might be destroyed, Mr. Weiss kept calling police until someone finally listened and promised to check out the gun. Sure enough, the tagged gun was still there at police headquarters. And, amazingly, when tested by ballistics experts, the long-barreled Buntline special revolver, which looked like a pistol from the Old Wild West, was proven to be the same weapon used at the Tate mansion. The killers had apparently tossed the murder weapon into the Weiss' yard while making their hurried escape.

In 1970, the band of killers was finally captured, and young Steven Weiss was called upon to testify in front of a packed courtroom. When Steven explained how he was careful to handle the gun to preserve fingerprints, but that the policeman picked it up "with both hands, all over the gun," the courtroom broke out in laughter.

The killers of Sharon Tate and her friends were convicted and sentenced to very long prison terms (some are still in prison even today, more than 40 years later). Steven Weiss was eventually awarded $1,000 of the posted $25,000 reward money for his sharp-eyed, sharp-witted help in bringing the dangerous killers to justice.

Important! If you ever happen to find a gun that has been dropped or tossed away, it is probably best not to try handling it yourself. Tell a trusted adult immediately, and have the adult call for the police.

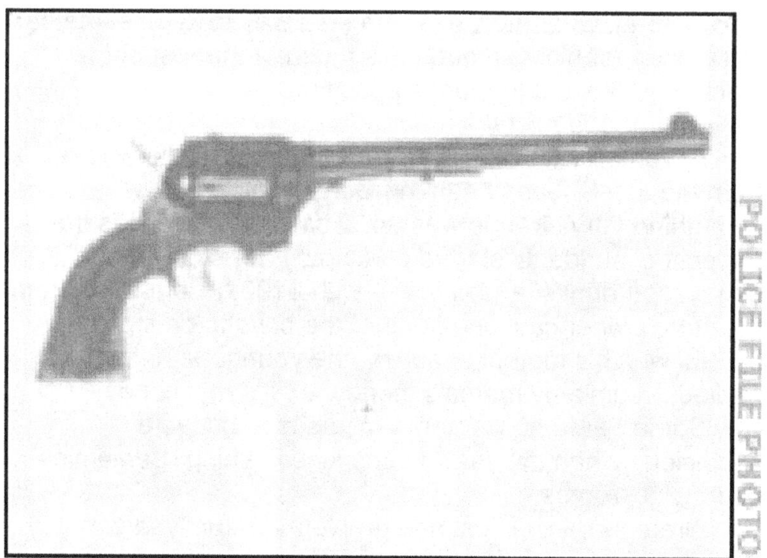

POLICE FILE PHOTO

Like Taking Candy from a Gangster

This is a story about what ***NOT*** to do with found treasure.

Back in January, 2005 an elementary school student somehow got hold of a bag containing a very considerable amount of money — at least $30,000 and possibly as much as $100,000. Where, how, and under what circumstances the money was found is still unknown. What is known is the money was discovered in a very poor, very rough section of Dallas, Texas.

So, did the young school kid turn the money over to his parents? Or maybe call police?

Most definitely not.

Instead, what the young man did was to keep some of the money for himself, and pass much of the rest of the stack of $100s out to friends at school.

Uh oh, *bad mistake*.

A woman who runs the snack shop and grille across from the J.J. Rhoads Learning Center quickly knew something very strange was up. That's because kids from the school suddenly started coming by her store to buy candy, soft drinks, and chips — with $100 dollar bills! When the store owner cautioned one of the boys to be more careful with his mother's money, the youngster defiantly replied, "It ain't my mama's money . . . it's my money!"

Some Learning Center teachers also became suspicious when they saw young kids flashing "Benjamins" in the classrooms.

Great fun — but just one problem. Actually, a very *big* problem. Seems the found money had been lost by some local men who were known to have very bad reputations. Gangsters, so the story goes, who had supposedly made the money illegally — most likely by selling drugs.

And now the gangsters wanted *their* money back.

It wasn't hard to figure out in a poor neighborhood who had the money. It was the kids with brand new basketball sneakers and jackets using $100 bills to purchase munchies.

Soon, the bad guys came knocking. First at school, and then at night at the kids' houses.

One of the men knocked on the door of a 12-year old boy, and put his hand in his jacket pocket as if he were holding a gun. "I don't have no problem with killing you," he yelled at the startled child. "I want my money right now."

Another boy got picked up off the street and taken for a very scary car ride. The bad guys smacked him around pretty good in the automobile's back seat, threatening the youngster to come clean. When he "fessed up" and told the men he'd spent some of the money and gave more away, they let the frightened youngster go.

Soon, half the neighborhood was hiding out, and hundreds of kids decided to stay home from school. Fear gripped the streets of South Dallas as gangsters spread out looking for their money — and the kids they thought had their money.

Police arrested one man in connection with the second boy's beating. According to the suspect, the money had been his — about $30,000 — honestly earned by fixing up and selling houses in the neighborhood. This "entrepreneur" claimed the money had been stolen from inside one of the houses he owned and was in the process of repairing.

"If someone's got your money," explained the man's sister, "wouldn't you want your money back?"

Police held the man on $5 million in bail, and ordered tight security in and around the neighborhood school. It was a long time before things got back to normal in South Dallas.

At last report, the police had no additional suspects, and were trying to get to the bottom of who found the money and where.

None of the school kids were charged or arrested.

Remember, treasure kids, if you find something of value, be smart, be responsible, and be honest. . . .

And don't be flashing $100 bills at your local convenience store when you get the munchies.

Duh!

Searching for Sediba

Having a father who is a paleoanthropologist must be quite a cool thing. Nine-year old Matthew Berger, whose father's job is to hunt for the fossilized remains of ancient humans, can definitely testify to that.

In 2008, Professor Lee Berger, an American scientist attached to the University of the Witwatersrand in South Africa, decided to concentrate his search for fossils along a series of hills about 50 miles north of Johannesburg, that country's capital. Professor Berger was looking for the homes of ancient cave dwellers. Although he hadn't had much success so far, the scientist had walked many miles in and around the Malapa Nature Reserve. The reserve is an area where previous researchers had discovered the remains of long-dead hominids (a class of bipedal creatures which includes recent human beings, our ancestors, and related species of primates). The region has been appropriately nicknamed "The Cradle of Humankind."

To narrow his search, Professor Berger used a very modern and easy-to-get tool. The American used the Google Earth software program to study the Malapa countryside, looking for shadows and distortions on his computer screen that may signify yet undiscovered caves, including the telltale clusters of trees that often mark their entrance.

On August 15, 2008, the professor brought along his Rhodesian ridgeback dog, Tau, to aid in the hunt. Also accompanying the scientist that day was Dr. Job Kibii, Berger's postdoctoral student. And, the scientist's nine-year old son, Matthew Berger, also tagged along. Early on, Professor Berger and Dr. Kibii found a cave, one that appeared previously undiscovered and unknown to scientists.

However, with his dad becoming preoccupied with work, Matthew engaged Tau in a bit of horseplay. This resulted in Matthew chasing his big dog down a dirt road and into the brush, where Matthew promptly tripped over a log. As he fell, the boy landed directly beside an odd-looking rock. Picking up this curious rock, young Matt quickly realized it contained a fossil. Off Matt ran to show his father.

"Dad!" Matt hollered. "I think I found a fossil!"

Professor Berger came out to see what the fuss was about, glimpsed his son holding the fossil, and began yelling at the top of his lungs like a crazy person.

Poor Matthew thought his father was angry, and that he was in serious trouble for doing something wrong. But the professor was not shouting because he was angry. No, the professor was shouting because he couldn't believe what his son was holding in his hands. It was simply too good to be true.

Matt was holding the clavicle (collarbone) of an ancient type of human being. Upon examining the rest of the rock, Professor Berger (who had years before wrote his thesis about the human clavicle) also found the mandible (lower jaw) and two teeth belonging to the same long-deceased individual.

In March, 2009, Professor Berger and colleagues found the skull belonging to the same creature Matt had discovered. They also found the skeleton of a woman about 30 years of age.

Close examination of the remains showed them to be approximately 1.78 to 1.95 *million* years old. They represent a newly discovered species, a being that was part ape but also surprisingly part human. Professor Berger was given the honor of naming this previously undiscovered species: *Australopithecus sediba.* "Sediba" is a local African word meaning wellspring or fountain.

Many scientists are today calling young Matt's find "one of the greatest fossils ever to rock the *paleoanthropological* world."

That's heavy praise for anyone, let alone a nine-year old boy.

Professor Berger and his fellow researchers are busy piecing together the evidence they've already collected. Much more needs to be done, and further discoveries are expected from the amazingly fossil-rich site at Malapa. Meanwhile, the professor believes that the boy and young woman came to the site to find much-needed water, probably during a period of severe drought. But the cave, which today is all but eroded away, was very steep two million years in the past.

The woman and the boy apparently fell down into the deep hole. The fall injured or possibly even killed them outright. Trapped in the deep cave, they perished. A later storm washed their bodies deeper into the cave, dumping them into a lime-rich sediment that acted much like cement, encasing their remains in a prison of hardening rock. Later the cave roof fell in, sealing the tomb for eons.

Other creatures found at the site have included saber-toothed cats, antelopes, mongooses, wild dogs, and hyenas. They too were lured to their deaths in the hole, thirsty with the promise of cool, fresh water that only spelled their doom.

So far, scientists have been unable to determine if the woman and young boy, who would have been 9-13 years old (approximately Matt's age), are in fact mother and son.

What they have determined is these ancient hominids, from a side-branch that did not lead directly to modern people, are a "fascinating" mix of primitive and advanced features. Like us, *Australopithecus sediba* had a small, humanlike face and walked on two legs. But they also had long arms for climbing trees, and brains that were approximately 1/3 the size of the brains belonging to people living today.

About 100 years ago, miners looking for limestone deposits placed dynamite in the eroded cave, blowing it wide open in order they might reach the money-making lime. Lime, an important chemical, is used in many products and materials such as paper, sugar, steel, paint, plastics, and dozens more.

The rocky material blown up in the cave was hauled out and used to fill in the dirt road that gave people access to the cave. Once the buried lime was gone, the cave was forgotten. Forgotten until, a nine-year old boy, chasing his dog, stumbled upon the unusual fossil rock which had been blown out from inside the old cave.

And then along came Sediba . . . an excellent candidate, as one expert put it, for being a transitional species. Another term for "transitional species" is the better known "*missing link,*" the dream discovery of anthropologists for decades.

This is a cave that will not be forgotten again in a long, long time. And most especially not by Matthew Berger, treasure kid and budding paleoanthropologist.

World's Greatest Treasure Hunt Ever!

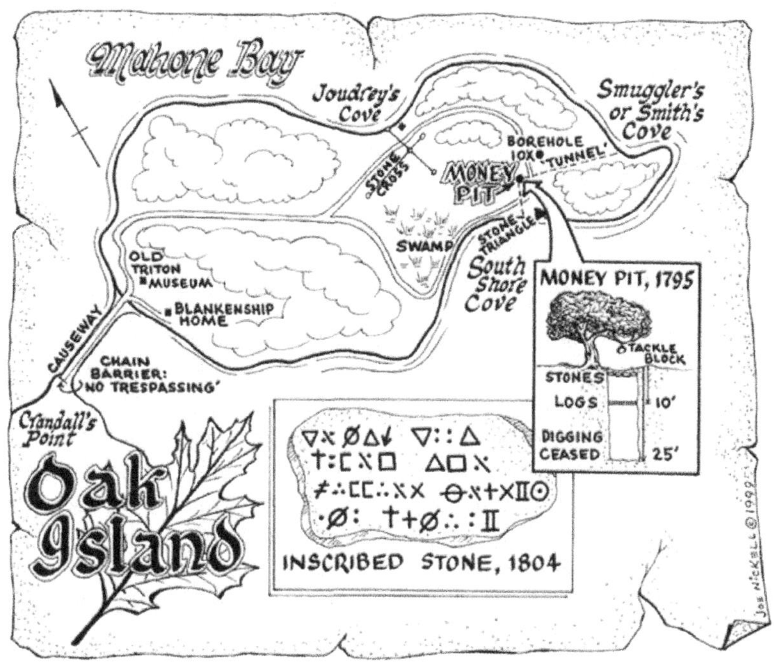

Source: oakislandtreasure.co.uk

We end this chapter of amazing adventures with a mystery. A very ***BIG*** mystery. It is a mystery that has endured for 215 years, and shows no signs of being solved any time in the near future.

In 1795, 16-year old Daniel McGinnis set off what would arguably become the world's most prolonged, expensive, and certainly most puzzling treasure hunt.

Is there treasure on Canada's Oak Island? If so, what is it, and who buried it there? Fortunes have been lost trying to unlock the island's secret. Six people have died in the attempt to reclaim the treasure from the so-called "Money Pit" . . . a treasure no one is certain ever existed.

Daniel began this long journey when he decided to row out to Oak Island, which sits just a few hundred feet offshore the Nova Scotia mainland. McGinnis and some of his pals had noticed strange lights sometimes glowing on the island after sundown. Until the teenager's discovery of unexplained strange goings on, Oak Island was a nondescript place, a small peanut-shaped island of 140 acres, one of hundreds of small islands lying in blustery Mahone Bay in the desolate far North Atlantic.

While exploring this nearby island, Daniel noticed a clearing near the isle's southeastern corner. And in that clearing stood a tree, a tree with a partially sawed off branch and the remains of a block-and-tackle pulley system for lifting and lowering heavy objects. Upon further inspection, Daniel discovered a 13-foot wide circular depression under the old tree branch. Someone had apparently dug a very large hole, lowered something large in that hole, and then once again filled the hole.

Daniel McGinnis had one thing on his mind — *buried treasure.*

Returning home, Daniel enlisted the help of two friends, fellow teenagers John Smith and Anthony Vaughn. Together, the three soon returned to Oak Island, prepared to unearth the buried prize.

Digging proved easy with the loosely filled-in dirt. At two feet down, the boys discovered a layer of flagstones. Thinking the treasure must be near, the boys dug faster. At ten feet they encountered their first mystery . . . a floor of oak logs. The boys removed the logs and kept digging, noticing the walls of the pit were scarred with pick markings. At 20 feet, a layer of oak logs and charcoal. At 30 feet, a layer of oak logs and putty.

The boys abandoned their frustrating search at 30 feet.

Eight years later in 1803, after having obtained the assistance of a businessman named Simeon Lynds, McGinnis, Smith, and Vaughn assisted with a newly formed treasure venture known as the Onslow Company.

The Onslow Company dug down to a depth of 90 feet, finding oak logs and other artifacts (such as coconut fiber, not normally found within 1,500 miles of Nova Scotia!) at each ten-foot level. Upon hitting a depth of 90 feet, the treasure hunters noticed the floor of the shaft was beginning to turn muddy. They also uncovered a mysterious stone slab with was inscribed by a series of ciphers (writing in code). Poking through the mud with a crowbar, they seemed to hit something solid. Could they be close to finding treasure? Retiring for the day, the fortune seekers retuned next morning, spirits high and anticipating a treasure find. To their utter amazement and disbelief, they found the 90-foot hole had filled back to a depth of 30 feet with some 60 feet of water!

Using buckets, the crew tried to bail out the water. To their disgust, they discovered no matter how fast they bailed, more water simply seeped into the pit.

Giving it one last try, the Onslow Company tried to dig a parallel shaft from which they could then dig sideways into the presumed treasure chamber. That parallel pit also soon filled with water!

Although the Onslow Company could make no further progress in reaching the purported treasure, someone did make headway in deciphering the mysterious stone slab and its strange markings. According to the code-breaker, the writing on the slab said:

FORTY FEET BELOW
TWO MILLION POUNDS ARE BURIED

= FORTY = FEET = BELOW
= TWO = MILLION
= POUNDS = ARE = BURIED

Two million English pounds in the 1700s would have represented a fortune of unbelievable size.

But 60 feet of seemingly impenetrable seawater stood in the way.

Someone, it appeared, had cleverly booby-trapped the shaft to fill with water once the treasure hunters got too close to the secret chamber.

Many years later, in 1849, the Truro Company would be the next to take an organized crack at the "Money Pit" Truro re-excavated back down to the 86-foot level, whereupon water started to seep into the shaft once again. Truro engineers built an ingenious platform above the water, from which their employees used an auger to drill down through the water and mud to the 98-foot mark. At 98 feet, the drill bit passed through a spruce platform. Then, 12 inches of dead air, followed by some 22 inches of what the drillers called "loose pieces of metal." Next, the drill supposedly passed through eight inches of solid oak, and then 22 more inches of metal, four more inches of oak, another layer of spruce, and then down into seven feet of clay without striking anything else. Reportedly, the drill bit pulled up what appeared to be small gold-colored links, as if from a gold chain.

Many people believed the Truro Company had drilled right through the heart of the treasure chamber. But despite their best efforts, Truro's treasure hunters weren't able to reach the prize down below.

Searchers did discover, however, that the site had been cleverly booby-trapped by five drains dug underground from nearby Smith Cove, some 500 feet away. Those drains diverted seawater towards the bottom of the Money Pit, causing the pit to fill with seawater whenever someone got too close to the buried treasure chamber.

The five drains, described as fanning out like five fingers on a hand, led back from the cove to a one main tunnel that consistently flooded the pit. The five fingers had been lined with sand and coconut fibers, which kept the hidden tunnel from becoming clogged.

Workers attempted to stop up the drains that fed the booby-trap tunnel, only to find that seawater began pouring in from the other side of the island!

In 1861, the Oak Island Association took over with an attempt to dig a parallel shaft and then "intersect" the secret chamber from the side. Their attempt caused a massive collapse of the Money Pit when water began seeping into the underground shaft, despite heroic attempts at a significant bailing operation. A loud crash was heard from the chamber, and it was supposed that the contents had fallen another 30 feet below — either into a hollow natural cavern or some new booby trap.

During the attempt to pump the rushing seawater to the surface, a boiler from a steam engine burst and killed a nearby worker. The unfortunate man would become the first fatality at Oak Island's Money Pit.

More attempts to reach the treasure followed throughout the later 1800s and early 1900s. In 1887, a second worker fell to his death while attempted to get at the treasure. In 1909, President Theodore Roosevelt was one of the participants working with the Old Gold Salvage Group. They too failed to pull a dime from the legendary Money Pit.

In 1931, William Chappel sank a 163-foot shaft close to the original pit. While digging, his crew allegedly found several ancient artifacts, including an axe, anchor fluke, and an old miner's pick. They also found a stone fragment with symbols similar to that found on the original cipher stone of 1803.

By the mid-1900s, searchers were having trouble locating the original McGinnis Money Pit, and the east end of Oak Island was beginning to resemble a giant slab of Swiss cheese. Many holes and piles of refuse littered the site from 150 years of ongoing treasure expeditions.

In 1940, action film star Errol Flynn, famous for his portrayal of Robin Hood, became interested in searching for the treasure of Oak Island. But when Flynn went to apply for a permit to dig for buried treasure there, he found the search rights were already owned by a company that belonged to Hollywood cowboy John Wayne!

In the early 1960s, tragedy struck Oak Island when four treasure seekers died while exploring a shaft near the original pit. The men were overcome by either by methane gas escaping from the pit, or by fumes from a gasoline-powered pump used to divert water from the shaft.

In 1965, Robert Dunfield used a 70-foot crane with a giant clam bucket to dig to a depth of 134 feet. Still, no treasure was found.

Triton Alliance tried next in 1967, excavating a 235-foot shaft down to the island's bedrock. They also reportedly lowered a camera down the shaft and into a previously undiscovered cave. According to the people running Triton, their searchers were able to recognize human remains, chests, and some tools. The camera's images were very murky, however, and have never been independently verified.

By the 1990s, strong disagreements between Mr. Daniel Blakenship and Mr. David Tobias, the Triton Alliance partners who had purchased the island, brought further exploration of the Money Pit to a standstill. Recently some investors from Michigan purchased Mr. Tobias' 50% interest in Oak Island, and there is that the new partners will be able to work with Blakenship to successfully resume the search . . .

A search that continues after some 215 years. Yes, 215 years — marked by greed, folly, frustration, and even death. And it all began back in George Washington's day with a 16-year old Nova Scotia youth who decided to row out to a deserted island for a little adventure.

There is a longstanding rumor about Oak Island. A local legend of sorts that says the treasure won't be found until every last oak tree on the island has been cut down, and that seven treasure hunters have died in their quest for fortune.

Today, one lone oak tree remains. And six fortune seekers have so far met an untimely end . . . searching for treasure no one is sure even exists. Treasure that is little more than speculation and imagination.

After 215 years, the ultimate treasure may lie in solving this enduring riddle. Who built this elaborate "money" pit — and why?

Was there ever treasure buried at depth? Is it still there, this "two million pounds buried forty feet below" the 90-foot level? Was the treasure long ago removed?

Some say it was Caribbean pirates the likes of Blackbeard or Captain Kidd. Others have suggested the Knights Templar hiding a valued religious artifact — perhaps the Holy Grail or the Ark of the Covenant itself. Or the precious jewels of ill-fated Marie Antoinette. Or even the golden spoils of a wrecked Spanish galleon. Then there's the tale of Francis Bacon, secretly burying evidence of his authorship of the plays allegedly written by William Shakespeare. Or the one about the secret vault of the Freemasons. Or the theory about wandering Vikings lying to rest one of their storied kings.

And most fanciful, perhaps, the idea that the Money Pit was constructed by the much fabled, mythic founders of Atlantis.

A skeptical few have even dared to suggest the entire affair was little more than an elaborate hoax. Or worse, a sinkhole caused by nature, into which a few downed trees and unusual man-made objects were dropped.

So, what's your theory? Everybody seems to have one when it comes to Canada's world-famous Money Pit.

To quote Winston Churchill, "It's a riddle, wrapped in a mystery, inside an enigma."

And maybe that's just the way it should stay.

UPDATE: Brothers Rick and Marty Lagina, from Michigan, are now digging on the island in an attempt to retrieve the treasure. Their quest is the subject of a of a popular cable television show, *The Curse of Oak Island*. Will Rick and Marty Lagina find the treasure? Tune in to find out!

Chapter 6 ♦ Dynamite Discoveries

In this chapter you'll find stories about some of the most unusual and important discoveries ever made by kids. Their incredible finds include a 1,000-year old Native American bowl, a rare blue-eyed cicada, a neutron star, some "lost" lady bugs, a fish weir, and a seldom-seen tektite.

What's a fish weir? What the devil are tektites? And how in the heck did the lady bugs ever get lost? Well, you'll just have to read the next six stories to find out!

Young Hiker Discovers Ancient Indian Artifact

A Texas teenager made a surprise archaeological discovery in the spring of 2006 while hiking with classmates. The setting was the Gila Wilderness near the Gila Cliff Dwellings in southwestern New Mexico. Andrew Connell,

15, was along for the hike in Gila with schoolmates when the group heard what they thought was an owl in the forest. Leaving the path to investigate, the teenagers spread out. While searching for the owl, Andrew by chance happened upon a rock wall. At the base of the wall he noticed something quite out of the ordinary, something sitting in a little niche at the base of the wall, partially covered by rocks and oak leaves. It was a bowl, obviously ancient, and most likely left behind at that spot for a long, long time.

Andrew took a closer peek at the unusual bowl, then told trip leaders. The hike's leaders suggested the bowl be left where it was found, but took care to photograph the bowl, sketch a map, and jot down the GPS coordinates for Andrew's discovery. They reported the find to employees at the Gila National Forest visitor center. The group's smart thinking allowed archaeologists at the Gila Cliff Dwellings to interpret this Native American artifact in its original setting, with as little disturbance as possible.

"To find something intact where it's been for a thousand years is very unusual," commented Ms. Carol Telles, an archaeologist at Gila. "The fact it is so complete and that we are able to reconstruct it is very important."

The almost intact prehistoric bowl was later determined to have been made by the Mogollon people, a tribe that had once inhabited this area. This unique American Indian culture once lived in the Southwest (primarily New Mexico and Arizona) and Northern Mexico from approximately 150 A.D. until 1450 A.D. The Mogollon (pronounced "Mug-ee-yun") constructed dwellings called "pit houses." Pit houses were big, excavated holes in the ground with domed roofs made of mud, grasses, and dried mud resting on wooden posts. The Mogollon prospered as hunters and gatherers, but also tended to large irrigated fields in later years. For meat, these Native Americans hunted bison (whose range extended into the desert Southwest from the Great Plains).

Also, groups of Mogollon gatherers, carrying woven baskets, would climb the mountains to collect wild fruits and seeds. Perhaps the bowl Andrew Connell found was left behind by such a gathering party. The bowl's location was a significant clue for archaeologists, because it showed them how far Mogollon would travel from their cliff dwellings to accomplish daily chores.

Famous for their ceramics, the Mogollon people produced beautiful black-on white bowls, classic examples of America's fine prehistoric artwork. These cleverly painted bowls were richly decorated with pictures of people and animals alike, as well as bold geometric designs. They point to the rich ceremonial customs of the Mogollon.

The name "Mogollon" comes from Don Juan Ignacio Flores Mogollón, the Spanish governor of New Mexico from 1712 until 1715. The Mogollon Mountains are also named after Señor Mogollón.

The well-preserved Mogollon bowl found by 15-year old Andrew Connell, sent to Gila National Forest's offices in Silver City after its discovery, is now being studied and researched by experts. Early plans are for Andrew's bowl to be proudly displayed in a Southwestern museum or exhibit.

"It's a pretty big deal," said Ms. Telles, one of the Gila archeologists who got to examine the treasured 1000-year old bowl.

Mystery of the Lost Ladybugs

Scientists at Cornell University are asking for help from kids all across America. They need *your* help in solving the mystery of the lost ladybugs. Back in the 1980s, nine-spotted ladybugs (also known as lady beetles) were the most common type of ladybugs found across North America. Now, they are practically extinct, and the entomologists (bug scientists) at Cornell want you to help find them.

You can go to **LostLadyBug.org** to help. All you need to do is find ladybugs in your neighborhood, take photos of them, and send your photos to the scientists. That's it!

The scientists are asking for kids of all ages (and their parents) to be the "legs, hands, and eyes" of the researchers, who simply can't look in all the places that need to be checked for the rare types of ladybugs — especially the elusive, rapidly disappearing 9-spotted kind.

Scientists call the nine-spotted ladybug Coccinella novemnotata, or just C-9 for short.

In October, 2006 two kids from Arlington, Virginia found and captured the very first 9-spotted ladybug seen in the northeastern United States in ***14*** years! The discovery made by Jilene Penhale (11) and Jonathan Penhale (10) proved to be extremely important. It told the scientists that while the nine-spotted ladybug had become extremely rare, it was not yet extinct.

Then, in 2010, a six-year old girl from Oregon found an entire batch of nine-spotted ladybugs in her backyard. Alyson Yates (shown here with Dr. Losey) had heard about the Lost Ladybug Project when she saw an ad in *Ranger Rick* Magazine. Turns out Alyson had some of the 9-spotters right there behind her own home. The scientists at Cornell were so very happy, they flew across the country to Oregon so just they could collect 13 of the now rare nine-spotted bugs — to bring back to their laboratory in New York State. The entomologists are now studying the endangered bugs at their lab, hoping the little beauties will produce even more little nine-spotters.

Word is the scientists are also looking for the rapidly disappearing *two-spotters*, as well as several other rapidly declining native ladybugs. You can get the entire scoop by visiting **LostLadyBug.org.**

No one knows exactly why or how these once-common bugs are dying out. In 1989, the nine-spotted ladybug was named New York's official state insect. A few short years later, during the 1990s, the 9-spotter had disappeared from the Empire State. The disappearance was so fast, so unexpected, and so troubling, it left scientists baffled as to the cause. What happened? Why did the local ladybugs disappear? Where did they go?

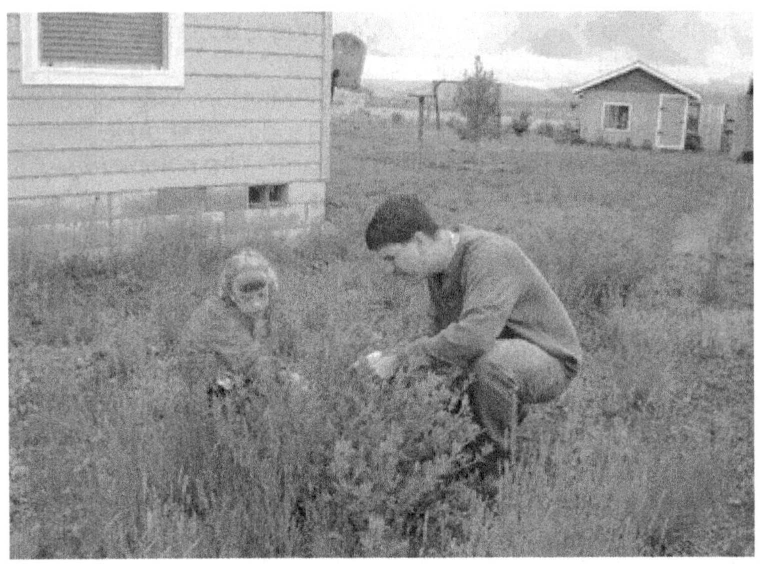

It is a puzzle entomologists now desperately race against time to solve.

Ladybugs of all types are extremely important in nature. First, they are very sensitive to the environment, and their demise may be signifying a small but important change in nature that scientists don't yet understand. Second, ladybugs are important because they eat small pests such as aphids and scales, the kind of pests that can destroy farmers' crops as well as flowers and plants that people raise in gardens.

About 450 species of ladybugs are native to the United States. There are perhaps 5,000 types of ladybugs across our planet. Many of those foreign bugs have arrived in North America (on trucks and ships and in cargo containers), and are quickly displacing the native ladybugs from their local habitat. If you see a ladybug today, it is more likely to be an Asian ladybug as opposed to one of the long-standing native varieties. Twenty years ago you would have likely been looking at a C-9. Some researchers think the new bugs have brought diseases that are hurting the North American ladybugs. Other scientists say the foreign bugs are better predators, more suited to compete for available food. Parasitic wasps, the enemy of ladybugs everywhere, are also high on the list of suspects. So are the many chemicals we produce in factories across the land, some which may be having unknown effects on our environment. Still other scientists believe a change in the nature of crops being planted by farmers has played an important role in the downfall of some beetles.

That's why the scientists need kids to help find the disappearing ladybugs — and find them before it's too late!

"All ladybugs are important," says John Losey, an entomologist at Cornell who heads the Lost Ladybug project. "Even if you don't find a rare bug, you can send in the photos."

Every ladybug photo, combined with an address for where the photo was taken, gives the scientists working with Dr. Losey a better idea of the distribution of lady bug types across the land. That means they can check bugs found in Pennsylvania against bugs found in Texas against bugs found in Florida against bugs found in Illinois against well, you get the idea. Every photo, every clue, gives scientists a better idea of the numbers and range for these insects.

Which means kids *everywhere* can help — even if you are in Canada or elsewhere in North America.

And, who knows, treasure kids, maybe you'll be the next person to find that rare, thought-to-be-extinct ladybug. The lucky person just like siblings Jilene and Jonathan Penhale from Arlington, Virginia. Or six-year old Alyson Yates from Oregon.

The truth is, you won't know until you look!

Georgia Boy Picks Up One Weird Space Rock!

A Georgia boy out for a day of fishing discovered a rock from space that was so unusual, a Cape Canaveral scientist, Mr. Hal Povenmire, decided to write a paper about it. Mr. Povenmire presented his findings at a NASA conference in Houston.

In the year 2000, 11-year old Daniel Brown was fishing with his grandfather on the Savannah River, when he happened to spot a very strange-looking disc-shaped stone. The odd stone was sitting on top of a sandbar poking out of the water. Daniel plucked the rock off the sandbar and carried it home, curious about what he had found.

"It looked like a piece of melted plastic," noted Daniel's grandfather. But it wasn't plastic — it was a rock. The specimen weighed about an ounce, with a blackened, glassy appearance that turned a greenish color when held up to a light. This rock was definitely something out of the ordinary. "It was just different, so I kept it," said Daniel.

Further investigation determined that Daniel had stumbled across a ***tektite***, a rare form of meteorite found only in the state of Georgia, a certain portion of Southeastern Asia, Australia, the Ivory Coast in Africa, and in Czechoslovakia.

Hey, but wait a minute. If meteorites fall from the sky, how come these tektites don't fall randomly across the globe . . . and in *every* country? The answer lies in the bizarre way the tektites fell to Earth ("tektite" is from the Greek word tektos, which means *molten* or "melted").

Scientists have two very different theories about tektites. Theory One says tektites are originally from Earth. Theory Two says they come from the Moon. Based on their special chemical composition and distinct formulation (tektites contain almost zero moisture), scientists unanimously agree that unlike most meteorites, tektites did not zoom around in deep space for billions of years before striking our planet. But exactly what caused these mysterious tektites is a matter of heated debate in the world of science.

Theory One says molten tektites were the result of asteroids or giant meteorites, in our very different past, slamming into Earth (*millions* of years ago). The impact and resulting explosions were so devastating, Earth rock was instantly melted and blasted up into space! Some of that melted rock eventually cooled, fell back into Earth's orbit, reentered the atmosphere, where it got heated up again, and crashed to Earth — much like any regular meteorite. Only they were Earth rocks first, melted and hurled up into space, which then fell back to Earth. Georgia tektites are supposed to have come from the terrific blast, hundreds of miles away, which carved out Maryland's Chesapeake Bay (think about *that* next time you bite into a delicious crab cake sandwich!). Tektites from other parts of the world supposedly came from other ancient craters.

Theory Two, however, says tektites have a *lunar* origin. Great volcanoes once erupted on the surface of the Moon, spewing liquid-hot lava into space (remember, the Moon has low gravity). Some of that molten moon lava froze in space, then naturally got pulled into nearby Earth's orbit, where it fell to the surface of our planet. Not your typical meteorites, but meteorites nevertheless. Mr. Povenmire is one of the scientists who believe Theory Two represents the actual truth. "It seems fanciful, and hard to conceive of, but that is the one (the theory) that is probably correct," Mr. Povenmire stated.

Well, who is right and who is wrong? Only time (and the discovery of more tektites, such as Daniel's) will tell. About 1,500 tektites have been found in Georgia over the past 30 years. Daniel's tektite was significant not only because it was one of the larger tektites found, but also because it was a surprising 40 miles northeast of where most Georgia space rocks are discovered. This means

Daniel Brown's discovery increased the known "strewn field" for the fall of these unique meteorites.

Perhaps someone else will find another tektite, and expand the known Georgia strewn field (area in which meteorites are known to have fallen) even more. Meanwhile, Mr. Povenmire requests that, "If you find a glassy object that appears black on the ground but greenish when you hold it up to the light, I hope you contact me!"

That's something to remember, treasure hunters.

Blue vs. Pink!

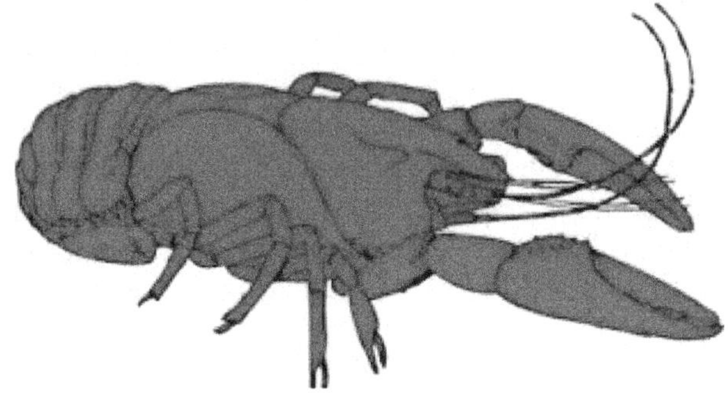

In July, 2006 some kids in Oneida County, Wisconsin were enjoying summertime at a local lake when they made a very unusual discovery. The kids found and captured a very uncommon, dazzling blue crayfish. The Wisconsin Department of Natural Resources confirmed that the crayfish (sometimes also called a crawdad or crawfish) was quite rare. Crayfish are normally a greenish-orange color, which helps keep them camouflaged. A local biologist who examined the creature remarked it was the first blue crayfish he'd ever seen in that part of Wisconsin, and that the animal's unusual color was probably hereditary.

The boy who found the crayfish kept it, and was going to have his uniquely colored trophy preserved.

Then, a year later in 2007, a six-year old suburban Chicago boy made what was described as a "one-in-a-million" find. Nicholas Wagner had heard a story in his kindergarten class about the rare blue-eyed cicada. The big winged insects are normally known for their fiery red eyes, not blue. But young Nicholas looked and looked in his family's garden, seeing many cicadas with the usual red eyes. Then, one day he finally found that elusive blue-eyed cicada. Nicholas picked it up and brought the strange-looking bug inside his house to show his mom.

Mr. Gene Kritsky, author of a book about cicadas, said that the bug's startling blue eyes were caused by a rare genetic variation. "It's indeed one-in-a-million," the author confirmed. "But then, there are hundreds of millions of cicadas!"

But in 2009, an 11-year old British schoolboy topped them all by finding a shockingly pink grasshopper. Not just the eyes pink . . . the entire grasshopper was pink!

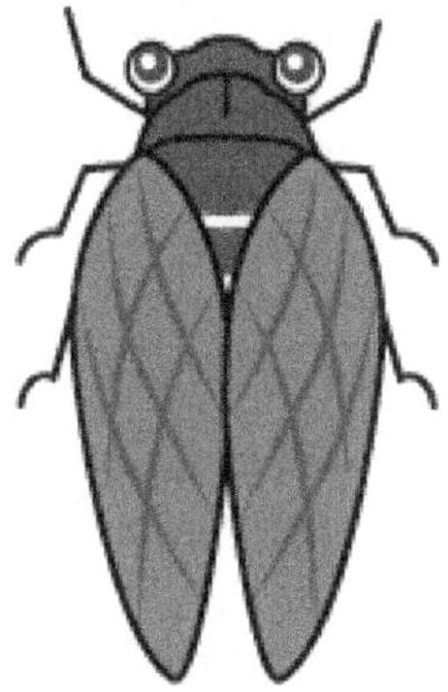

Daniel Tate was attending a wildlife event at Seaton Marshes Local Nature Reserve in England when he made his discovery. Daniel was looking for grasshoppers — but certainly not the pink kind! "I saw something pink, and I thought it was a flower," explained the boy, "but then I saw it move." When he saw it jump, Daniel knew he had a grasshopper.

Park officials quickly identified Daniel's catch as an adult female common green grasshopper . . . except this insect was pink. *Very, very* pink.

Mr. Fraser Rush, a nature reserves officer, said there are millions of common green grasshoppers, but that he had never seen such a pink one before. Sometimes this animal can be different shades of green and brown, or even slightly purple. But not Mary Kay Cosmetics pink!

Pink grasshoppers are not entirely unheard of, but what made Daniel's grasshopper so spectacular was the vivid intensity of its pink shade.

Mr. Rush noted there was a chance that Daniel's shockingly pink grasshopper might have given birth to more grasshoppers and passed her unusual gene along. Park employees will be on the lookout for more gloriously pink specimens.

Rare examples of pink praying mantises, dragonflies, katydids, and humming bird moths have also been reported.

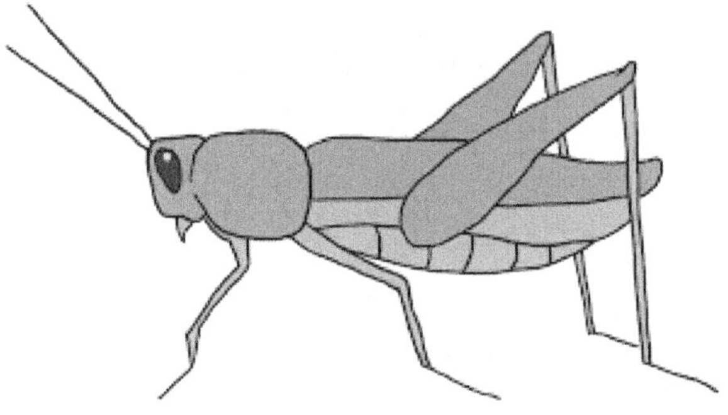

No Ordinary Rock!

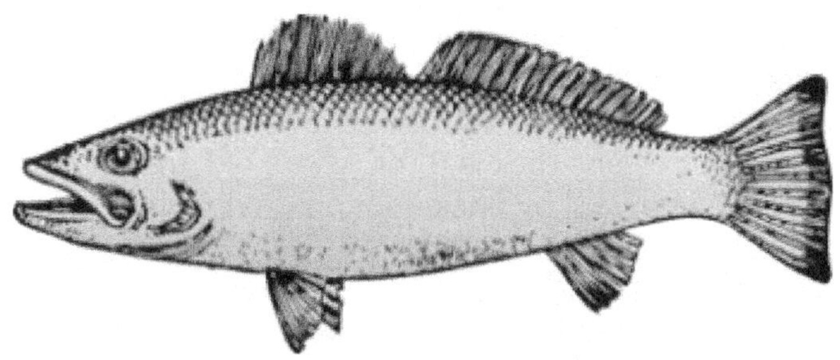

Summers are usually short in the cold, rocky, northern state of Maine. Residents of Maine learn to make the best of warm weather while it lasts. Six-year old Tyler Levesque has certainly been no exception to this rule. During the summer of 2006, young Tyler much enjoyed visiting nearby Sebasticook Lake with his mom and dad, having just learned to swim the year before in 2005. The Levesque family would often go boating, or sometimes just relax along the northeastern shore, close by their home in the town of Newport. Tyler, fond of using a swim mask, would dive for rocks at the bottom of the lake. One day Tyler dove down into Lake Sebasticook and came popping up holding a slightly sort of unusual looking rock. "I knew it was special right away," explained Tyler. "It had kind of a hole in it." Tyler's dad didn't think his son's rock looked all that particularly significant. However, when Tyler showed the rock to his mom, she quickly agreed with Tyler.

The rock definitely seemed to have some sort of history. Someone had made that hole on purpose.

Well, guess what, Tyler and Mrs. Levesque were absolutely 100% correct. An archaeologist from the University of Maine got a chance to examine Tyler's rock — and the scientist *certainly* thought Tyler's rock was very special. The archeologist quickly identified the rock with the hole as a "gouge." It was a piece of hardware that Native Americans shaped by hand to use on something called a "fish weir." A fish weir was an old-style fish trap that, when stretched across the mouth of a river, would catch lots of fish that came swimming downstream.

Turns out Tyler's rock is 6,000 years old, the strange hole being carved out by ancient people living near Lake Sebasticook very, very long ago.

"It's older than the pyramids," observed Dr, Brian Robinson while examining Tyler's rock.

Fish weirs were built by uprooting saplings and small trees, then using them as posts at the point where a river entered a lake. In this case, Lake Sebasticook. Native Americans would then weave a net made from tree branches, and string this net-like fence underwater between the posts. Think of someone lowering a soccer goalpost across the narrow point in a creek — the effect would basically be the same. Fish would swim into the underwater net and get tangled . . . eventually becoming lunch for the locals. The "gouge" with its hole was used to scrape and shape those sturdy posts that held the fish weir in place. Remember, 6,000 years was well before Loews and Home Depot arrived on the scene! People had to make do with what they could find or make — without fancy power tools or anyone else's help.

The Sebasticook fish weir, parts of which still lie hidden for most of the year under the waters of Lake Sebasticook, was identified and dated in 1992. This official finding was made by Dr. James Peterson, an archaeologist from the University of Maine. A very small number of other fish weirs (only three) have been discovered in other areas of North America (Canada and the United States), but the Sebasticook site is the *oldest* known and best preserved.

In an official ceremony held by the Newport Historical Society, Tyler Levesque was honored for making his amazing discovery. Tyler was also applauded for donating this ancient stone tool to the historical society.

"This is part of one of the most important things in Newport," remarked Newport Historical Society President Ron Hopkins, describing the gouge once used to help build the town's 6,000-year old fish weir. "We can't thank you enough, Tyler." smiled Mr. Hopkins, praising the young man before him who had discovered this unusual stone artifact.

Today, the town of Newport displays Tyler's gouge, along with replicas made of the fish weir posts, at the Newport Cultural Center. The fish weir artifacts are joined by a host of other interesting artifacts and objects from the historical society's impressive collection.

If you are lucky enough to visit Maine, be sure to stop by and see Tyler's now-famous rock!

Kids Use New Technologies to Make Discoveries in Space

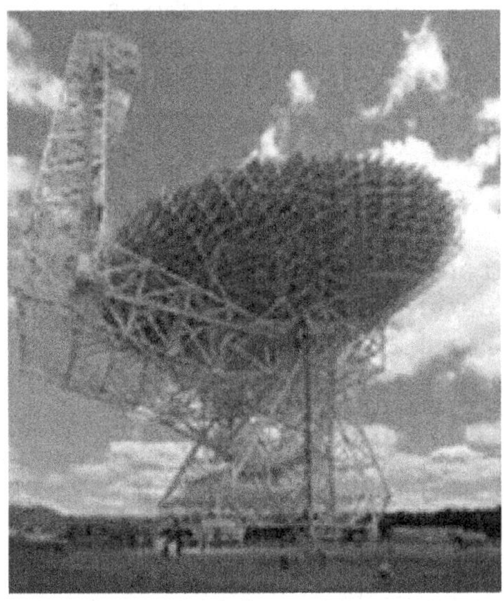

In 2007, folks at the National Radio Astronomy Observatory in West Virginia came up with a very interesting program. Their enormous Green Bank Telescope, a space-aged monster weighing almost 17 million pounds, was busy capturing data from the sky in such vast amounts that scientists could no longer study or keep up with all of the incoming information. So, using a grant from the National Science Foundation, the Pulsar Search Collaboratory (PSC) and West Virginia University decided to train school kids and their teachers to analyze some of the data collected by the enormous eye on the sky.

The kids' mission? To find evidence of new, undiscovered pulsars. A pulsar, known also as a neutron star, is actually a giant galactic corpse. Pulsars are the "dead bodies" of exploded stars that burned out during fiery supernovas. Having collapsed in on themselves, the small, dark, dense pulsars rotate out in deep in space, radiating beacons of radio beams — pulses. Think of a lighthouse shooting a rotating beam of light into the night sky. Well, pulsars work much the same way — only they blast out *radio beams* while spinning through space.

Astronomers gave the kids from several West Virginia schools some special software used to analyze the telescope's data. Plus, they taught students and their teachers how to distinguish the ordinary radio waves from Earth . . . man-made interference that might distract kids from finding the hidden pulsars.

So, how did the kids do? Well, so far, absolutely great!

In 2009 came news that Lucas Bolyard, 16, had found evidence of a rare type of pulsar known as a radio transient. Only 30 of these odd collapsed stars have ever been discovered — *one by Lucas*! "I saw a plot with a pulse," explained the high school sophomore from Clarksburg, West Virginia. "But there was a lot of interference. The pulse almost got dismissed as interference."

Later, scientists checked Lucas' data, and determined he had indeed found a radio transient. Radio transients are quirky types of pulsar that shoot radio beams for a time and then stop — only to "pulse" again later. Astrophysicists don't know what makes radio transients act the way they do. Lucas' discovery may provide part of the answer.

Okay, think that's not a big deal? Well, think again. Lucas was invited to be the guest of honor at the White House's October, 2009 "star party." The young man was introduced to the crowd by non-other then President Obama, who explained to attendees what Lucas had discovered, and why it was important.

Then, less than a week after the White House party, 15-year old Shay Bloxton of Summersville, West Virginia amazed astronomers by finding a new pulsar some 26.8 million billion miles from Earth. "Participating in the PSC has definitely encouraged me to purse my dream of being an astrophysicist," Shay told news reporters after her discovery was announced.

Not to be outdone, a group of California seventh-graders were credited in 2010 with discovering a strange, new cave — on Mars! The West Coast students were able to locate their Martian cave through a research project for kids. The program allows kids to study images taken by NASA's Mars orbiter. Under the Mars Student Imaging Project, participating kids devise a group question about the red planet . . . and then arrange to have the Mars camera pointed at a particular surface feature. The camera images might then be used to answer the students' question.

At Evergreen Middle School in Cottonwood, California, 16 kids in a science class decided to find out more about Martian lava tubes. Lava tubes are also found on Earth — The Big Island of Hawaii is famous for its lava tubes. These types of tubes are hollow tunnels in rock that were carved out by molten lava flows from a volcano. The tubes later cooled and hardened, becoming permanent.

The kids at Evergreen posed an interesting question: are lava tubes on Mars found mostly on the summits of volcanoes, on the sides of volcanoes, or in the flat lava fields on the plains beside volcanoes?

The seventh graders submitted their question, and the Mars orbiter was later positioned to take photos of the Pavonis Mons volcano on that planet. The two photos sent back (a primary photo plus backup) were taken with a special imaging device known as THEMIS (Thermal Emission Imaging System).

When the seventh graders got their photos of Pavonis Mons, they included several lava tubes surrounding the volcano — just as the kids had anticipated. But one of those photos showed something peculiar. One of the giant Martian lava tubes appeared to have a black hole in its roof. Collapsed tubes were common — but an intact tube with its very own skylight? Now *that* certainly seemed to be something extraordinary.

Glen Cushing, a scientist with the U.S. Geological Survey, caused some excitement in 2007 when he found the first such Martian "skylight" using THEMIS. The scientist published a paper about the tube caves, which seem to be cooler than the surrounding surface area during Martian days, but warmer during the frigid Martian nights. After looking at the lava tube cave discovered by the California seventh-graders, Mr. Cushing agreed this was a previously unknown skylight, and only the second one found at the Pavonis Mons volcano. Mr. Cushing estimated the kids' cavern to be 380 feet deep and 620 by 520 feet wide.

Scientists at the Mars Space Flight Facility in Tempe, Arizona have plans to use a special camera from their High Resolution Imaging Science Experiment (HiRise) to get a more detailed look inside this mysterious black hole. The high resolution camera is aboard NASA's Mars Reconnaissance Orbiter, and may provide new clues as to the nature of the skylight. Also, what might be lying inside that football stadium-sized hole in that gigantic lava tube — tens of millions of miles from Earth!

Meanwhile, teacher Dennis Mitchell spoke for his 16 very excited science students when he praised the Mars Student Imaging program. "It's certainly one of the greatest educational programs ever developed," observed Mr. Mitchell. "This has been a wonderful experience!"

Chapter 7 ♦ Lost and Found

Some of the best treasure finds made by kids are of valuable items that need to be returned to their rightful owners. The following are true stories about some kids who stepped up and did the right . . . and who were usually rewarded for their honesty. Remember, being a finder doesn't necessarily mean you should always be a keeper. In case of a recently lost item, we all have a duty to try to return it into the hands of the proper owner. Sometimes the best reward can be the amazed smile on a disbelieving owner's face!

Boy Finds a Bundle While Bagging Groceries!

Paper or plastic? That's the decision most supermarket grocery baggers have to make dozens of times every day. But that routine changed for one young grocery clerk who made a very unusual on-the-job discovery one November evening in the state of Washington.

In 2008, the Federal Way, Washington high school senior was earning minimum wage by bagging groceries and sweeping floors at his neighborhood supermarket. Moisei Baraniuc, who goes by the nickname Moses, was busy one night at Top Food & Drug when he decided to take a quick break to wash his hands. As he stepped into the men's restroom at the market, 17-year old Moses suddenly noticed a brown canvas bag lying on the floor, no apparent owner in sight. Curious, Moses reached down and opened the bag. That's when he saw the envelopes crammed with money. Lots and lots of money.

"It was a pretty thick stack," Moses would say in a later interview.

Moses set the bag down on the counter as he washed his hands, thinking about what to do with this bag stuffed full with $100s and $50s. Moses would later admit that he thought about keeping all that cash — but only for a split second. Moses then thought about all the little kids he taught in Sunday school at the First Ukrainian Baptist Church. It would be a bad example for them if Moses kept the money. And then there was Moses' father, Mr. Vitalie Baraniuc, who brought his family here to the United States from Moldava in 2003. At that time the Baraniucs only had $300 to their name, and a burning dream to live in America.

"You've got to work for yourself," Mr. Baraniuc told his son. "If you take what doesn't belong to you, it will catch up to you."

With these things in mind, Moses took the bag and handed it into his boss, Suanne Schafer. Ms. Schafer and another employee took the money to a quiet spot and starting counting. All $10,000 of it. Seems the brown canvas bag contained a total of *85* hundred-dollar bills and another *30* fifty-dollar bills.

That's a lot of mullah.

Ms. Schafer called the Federal Way Police, who couldn't believe someone had just found $10,000 in an abandoned bag — and was being honest enough to turn it in!

Police came and got the money. Hours later, a Mr. Fred Smith called the market, asking if anyone had found a bag with some cash. The Vancouver, Washington man accurately described the bag, the envelopes with totals written on them, and — most importantly — the 85 $100s, and 30 $50s. A receipt showing Mr. Smith had bought groceries that day at Top Food & Drug sealed the deal. The man got his money back, thanks to Moses. Seems Mr. Smith, who was in the process of moving, had placed the cash — his life savings — in the canvass bag for transport. But during the side trip to the supermarket the Vancouver man put the bag down on the bathroom floor and forgot about it.

Later that same week, Mr. Smith paid a visit to the supermarket to thank Moses personally. "I'll send you a little reward," the bag's owner promised Moses.

Good to his word, Mr. Smith soon sent Moses a check for $500!

But the story doesn't end there. Moses soon received another $500 check, this time from his employer, Top Food & Drug. Then even more checks started to come, including another $500 check from a stranger in Oregon. In all, people sent Moses Baraniuc more than $2,000 as their way of saying thanks for a job well done.

Students from a middle school in New Jersey wrote Moses 600 cards and letters of praise. ***600!***

Moses, using this as an opportunity to do more good, spent the money on taking a missionary trip to Ukraine during the summer of 2009.

In school we all learn the Golden Rule . . . "Do unto others as you would have them do unto you."

"What comes around, goes around" is another less formal way of saying much the same thing. By following the Golden Rule and setting an example for others, Moses Baraniuc was now receiving many blessings in return . . . and not all of them monetary.

Way to go, Moses.

Boy Scout Recovers Purse with 19 "Benjamins"

A Boy Scout in Greensboro, North Carolina was credited in December, 2009 with recovering a stolen purse containing $1,900. Edward Myers, 11, was helping his mother, siblings, and neighbors who were planting trees to help beautify a local Greensboro park. Edward and his mother went to the nearby creek in order to retrieve a bucket of water for the newly planted trees. That's when Edward and his mom spotted what appeared to be a discarded purse at the water's edge. Lowering himself down several feet onto a flat rock, Edward was able to successfully grab the purse and hand it up to Mrs. Myers. The purse was waterlogged, and appeared to have been lying outside in the elements for some time. Inside the lady's purse, Edward's mom found a wallet. There was no money in the wallet's side billfold, but when she opened up a zipper and explored further, she quickly found the money tucked away in another compartment.

"That's when I saw all the Benjamins!" exclaimed Donna Myers.

That's Benjamins as in Ben Franklins, better known as $100 dollar bills. There were nineteen "Benjamins" in all for a grand total of $1,900 in cold, hard cash.

Edward and his mother called the Greensboro Police. Police arrived momentarily and found a checkbook elsewhere inside the mystery purse. The checks contained the phone number of their owner, whom police immediately called. The lady soon arrived at the park to identify and claim her soggy purse along with the 19 equally soggy Benjamins. Seems someone had broken into the poor woman's car around Thanksgiving while the lady was visiting her daughter. The doofus thief or thieves found $30 in the wallet's side billfold. Then, thinking the purse and wallet were now empty, they quickly tossed them into the creek as they made a hasty getaway. But the wallet still contained 19 Benjamins in the unsearched compartment, the other spot the criminal genius or geniuses somehow neglected to check.

Duh!

As a reward, the grateful owner of the purse gave Edward one of those soggy Benjamins. Edward used the Benjamin to buy a Carolina Panthers football jersey for $60, and then he gave the $40 in change to his mother.

And yes this is all true, every word, Scout's honor!

Fifth-grade Girl Hits Home Run with World Series Ring

As the former scouting director for the National League Pittsburgh Pirates, 82-year old Merrill Hess was once paid to find hidden gems. But in 2010, an 11-year old New Jersey girl would make headlines by finding Mr. Hess' own lost gem — a prized 1960 World Series Ring!

In 1960, Hess was a young assistant scouting director for the upstart Pittsburgh Pirates, who managed to beat the highly favored New York Yankees in a thrilling seven-game series. The classic fall showdown was decided by a walk-off home run by legendary Pirates shortstop Bill Mazeroski. That 1960 series has long been considered one of the most exciting World Series in baseball history. Hess, just like Mazeroski and the rest of the team, was awarded a World Series ring for his efforts in helping to build a winning organization.

The ring, which would be greatly prized by any collector, was gold with diamonds shaped in the likeness of Forbes Field, the Pirates' home stadium back in 1960.

Treasure Kids!

Fast-forward 50 years to February, 2010 at an ice rink in Morristown New Jersey. The now 82-year old Hess somehow accidentally loses his prized ring while attending a high school hockey game. Two days later, Hess realizes his World Series ring is missing, and has no idea where he lost it. Mr. Hess and his wife call restaurants they've patronized, and turn their Morristown home inside-out looking for the irreplaceable memento. Sadly, they have no luck. Mr. and Mrs. Hess figure the ring is gone forever, probably lost on a recent trip to Florida.

"I was heartbroken," recalls Merrill Hess.

Then, along comes fifth-grader Kate Drury of nearby Chatham, N.J. Kate is there at the Twin Oaks Ice Rink one day to watch her brother play hockey. While stopping by the snack bar, Kate happens to spot a ring lying under a table. Kate takes the ring to her parents, who notify rink management. But no one has reported any missing ring to Twin Oaks employees.

Still, young Kate is determined to find the rightful owner of the unusual ring. Unfortunately, although there seems to be a name inscribed in gold, the ring is nearly a half century old, and the inscription is badly worn. Kate's best guess is the ring belongs to a person named "Merrill Mess." With Kate's curiosity kicking into high gear, she goes online and posts a question on Yahoo! Answers, asking if anyone might know the owner of this World Series ring. Soon after, Merrill Hess' grown daughter, Arlan, decides to use Google's popular search engine in a last-ditch effort to find news, *any news*, about her father's missing World Series memento.

Bingo! Arlan quickly finds Kate's Yahoo! Answers post and replies. Astonished to find she is communicating online with someone in elementary school, Arlan asks Kate to have Kate's parents contact her. Soon, the Drury family was making the six-mile drive to Mr. Hess' home in Morristown to reunite the retiree with his prized ring.

Mr. Hess was so thankful to young Kate that he presented Kate with a check, a gift certificate, and an autographed photograph from that classic 1960 World Series.

"This was a little girl doing the right thing," observed Mr. Hess' daughter, Arlan. "That ring could have paid for her freshman year in college!"

At last report, Mr. Hess was looking forward to attending the much-anticipated 50th reunion of his beloved world champion 1960 Pittsburgh Pirates.

Source: New Jersey's *The Star-Ledger*

Adopt a Highway, Take Home a Treasure

Ten year-old Arie Johnston of Dover, New Hampshire was just busy doing a good deed. While visiting his grandmother up north in Alton, New Hampshire in May, 2009, Arie decided to help his grandmom and the other citizens of Alton with the annual cleanup of their main road through town, Route 11. As Arie and his grandmom pitched in and assisted in picking up litter thrown by the side of the roadway, Arie happened to spot an abandoned backpack lying behind Route 11's guardrail. When Arie retrieved the backpack, which was charred as if having been in a fire, he realized there was still something inside. Arie took a quick peek and saw papers, a couple of passports, and cash.

Lots of cash. Arie had certainly expected to see lots of stuff on the side of the road that needed to be picked up — but not *treasure*! The Dover boy told his grandmother about what he had found, and she quickly called Alton's town clerk.

Based on the passports and other documents contained in the burnt pack, the clerk was able to identify the backpack's owner. She was a woman who used to live on Route 11 directly across the street from Arie's discovery. It seems the woman's apartment had been damaged in a fire in 2008, and she had since moved out of state.

When police counted all the cash in the backpack, it came to a grand total of $9,420. They contact the owner, who told police the money had come from an insurance settlement. Police believe the backpack and cash got thrown out either while firefighters were busy fighting the apartment fire, or afterwards when burnt and smoke-damaged items were being removed from the apartment. Then, when the long winter came to snowy New Hampshire, the pack got buried for months under a snow pile — probably from the busy Alton snowplows. It was there all those months just waiting for someone to come along in the spring and find it.

That someone happened to be the observant 10-year old Arie Johnston.

The backpack's owner asked police to turn the money over to her sister who was still living in Alton. When reporters talked to Arie's grandmother shortly after the money was returned, she told them a reward for Arie may be on the way.

Now there's one kid who sure knows how to clean up!

Toddler Recovers Precious Lost Jewelry

The prize for being the youngest treasure kid in this book goes to Ryan Baima, who was only *three* when he found gold in 2009. Ryan, who loves to dig, was shoveling merrily away in the backyard of his Franklin, Massachusetts home when he struck what the 49ers called "pay dirt." Holding up a gold engagement ring, young Ryan went over to his mother and presented the band to her. "Here, Mommy," said Ryan. "I found your ring."

Mrs. Luna Baima took the ring from her son and kindly thanked him, believing Ryan had found a fake ring someone had thrown away. Or, perhaps that Ryan had dug up an inexpensive old piece of long-forgotten costume jewelry. A few minutes later, however, Ryan returned and asked his mom, "Do you want another one?"

That "other one" proved to be a gold wedding band. Mrs. Baima was startled, realizing her son had just found someone's lost wedding ring *and* engagement ring. And Mrs. Baima was determined that, if she could find that person, the rings would be returned to their rightful owner. Whomever had lost them must be missing them terribly.

Doing some old-fashioned detective work, Mrs. Baima told neighbors about what Ryan had found. One neighbor, who had lived in Franklin many years, recalled a woman named Mrs. Joan Mulligan who had been the original owner of the house where Ryan now lived. She also recalled how Mrs. Mulligan had lost both her rings while gardening in the backyard — and even paid local children to help look for them.

But no, Mrs. Mulligan's rings had never been found.

With a little more detective work, Ryan's mother found where Joan Mulligan was living, and gave the now retired schoolteacher a phone call.

"I think I have something that belongs to you," said Mrs. Baima when the schoolteacher answered the phone. Even before Ryan's mom explained who she was and what it was Ryan had found, Mrs. Mulligan knew instantly this was about her long-lost rings.

The rings had been gone for 33 long years . . . they'd been lost in 1976!

Both Mrs. Baima and Mrs. Mulligan think it's a miracle the rings were recovered. Several truckloads of dirt had been removed from the Baima backyard just weeks before Ryan discovered the rings. The rings were actually found on the *other* side of the yard from where Mrs. Mulligan believes she lost them.

For decades, since the loss of her rings, Mrs. Mulligan had worn her mother's engagement and wedding rings. But she never forgot her own precious rings, the ones lost in her own backyard and never recovered.

Until 2009. . . .

Mrs. Mulligan, hardly believing her good fortune, took the rings to a jeweler to have them cleaned and repaired.

Treasure Kids!

Joan and Mr. Mulligan celebrated their 50th wedding anniversary in 2010 with the retired schoolteacher happily wearing all four rings! Her own rings a courtesy, of course, of Ryan's seemingly miraculous discovery.

For his reward, Mrs. Mulligan came to visit Ryan and Luna Baima in person, and gave the boy several $50 bills for his recovery of the precious treasure. Ryan was so happy it is said he danced around, whooping it up, tossing his crisp, new green "Grants" straight up into the air.

Let's hope treasure kid Ryan hangs on to those $50s, else some other kid will have to go digging them up in that backyard sometime in the distant future!

Treasure Girl Rides Summer Surf

In August, 2008, 11-year old Rowan Short was just trying to enjoy the remaining days of her summer vacation. Spending the day at the beach in Ocean City, Maryland with her family, Rowan decided to hop into the surf for a swim. But while enjoying the warm, relaxing ocean water, the Brandywine, Delaware girl felt something touch her foot. Curious, Rowan reached down under the surface and came up with a very wet Ziploc baggie. The baggie was filled with $20 dollar bills and $50 dollar bills. Lots of them.

Rowan brought the Ziploc baggie onshore and gave it to her mother. Mrs. Short opened the baggie and counted $1,070 in cash. There were also two credit cards and a Pennsylvania driver's license.

Using her cell phone, Mrs. Short dialed 411 to ask for the phone number of the man shown on the driver's license, a Mr. Michael Chosky from the Pittsburgh area. Within seconds, Mrs. Short had the Pennsylvania man on the line.

Treasure Kids!

Seems Mr. Chosky had just returned home with his wife, their vacation having ended on a very sour note. Mr. Chosky was convinced he'd never see his money, credit cards, or driver's license again. Michael and Elaine Chosky had gone to the beach the day before, some 15 blocks farther down the beach from where Rowan and family would arrive the next day. Years earlier, while Mr. Chosky had been vacationing in Florida, someone had swiped money he had left for the day in his hotel room. And since the hotel room Mr. and Mrs. Chosky had rented in Ocean City didn't have a safe where guests could store valuables, Mr. Chosky instead came up with another plan. The Pittsburgh area man instead stuffed his cash, his credit cards, and his driver's license into a Ziploc baggie, and slipped the baggie inside the Velcro-lined pocket of his swim trunks.

Only problem was, the surf got a bit rough that day. When Mr. Chosky waded out of the water, he was heartsick to discover the Ziploc baggie was gone.

Mr. and Mrs. Chosky were so thrilled to get the driver's license and credit cards back, they offered Rowan half the cash — $535! — as a reward. But after consulting with her parents, Rowan Short decided to accept the much more modest reward of $20.

But soon young Rowan got another surprise. Her photograph appeared on the *front page* of the *Wilmington News Journal* for all of Rowan's friends and neighbors to see. On the front page, next to a photograph of Delaware Senator Joe Biden no less, who would soon become the vice-President of the United States! And when Rowan began her first day in sixth grade, many of the school's teachers made it a point to congratulate Rowan for her honesty.

"Everybody saw the story," laughed Rowan later. "I didn't think it was going to be this big!"

Some rewards, as this Delaware girl discovered, can't simply be measured in dollars and cents.

Chapter 8 ♦ Serendipity

Webster's dictionary defines "serendipity" as the "faculty of finding valuable or agreeable things not sought for." Basically, finding treasure through good, old-fashioned *dumb luck*! Sometimes it is simply better to be lucky than good . . . and being in the right place at the right time can be very, *very* important. And so we give you a last chapter filled with stories about treasure kids blessed with the most amazing kinds of luck. Now remember, try not to be jealous, because the next bit of good fortune might hopefully be yours. . . .

Boy Discovers Rare Pearl — without Even Trying!

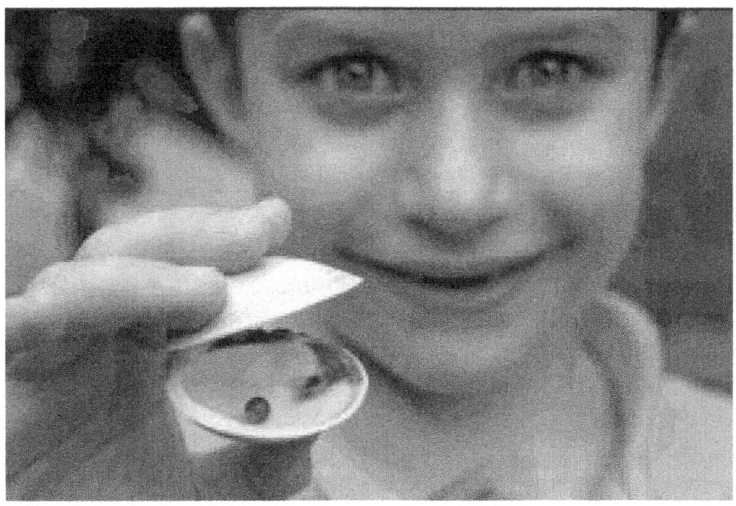

Seven-year old Conor O'Neal of Barrington, Rhode Island possesses an almost encyclopedic collection of facts about the ocean. Even though Conor was just about to enter first grade in later summer of 2009, his favorite subject was marine biology.

Not surprisingly, when it comes to food, young Conor also prefers a taste of the sea. In late August of 2009, Conor's mom, Ms. Mary Talbot, bought a batch of littleneck clams at a Barrington supermarket. When Conor's mom got home, she cooked up a batch of linguini and clams for Conor's lunch. Conor sat down and began eating when, uh oh, he bit into something really hard. Conor quickly spit the piece out, making sure he didn't swallow.

"I thought it was a pearl," said Conor.

And guess what . . . Conor was absolutely correct. The boy had just discovered — in his *lunch* no less, a beautiful purple-colored pearl!

Littleneck clams, the kind Conor has been so fond of eating, are also known as quahog clams. Littlenecks are the juvenile version of the adult quahogs. Pearls in quahogs are common enough, with pearls being formed in approximately one in every 500 such clams. But quahog pearls are generally whitish and not particularly colorful. According to Professor Michael Rice, who specializes in fisheries and aquaculture at the University of Rhode Island, a purple pearl from a quahog clam is "very, very rare."

Like diamonds, the size, color, and rarity of pearls ultimately helps to determine their value. Professor Rice noted that, "With a well-formed quahog pearl, there have been cases where pearls have been worth several hundred to a couple of thousand dollars." In other words, more than enough to buy lunch!

No news yet on how much money Conor's rare purple pearl may be worth, but his mother hopes to have it appraised and then to sell it. The profit from the sale of Conor's pearl will go into the boy's college fund.

Meanwhile, last report was that young Conor was keeping an eye on his lucky purple pearl by storing it in a

Ziploc bag. Asked if he would go looking for pearls in other clams, Conor replied that he didn't know if he liked looking for pearls (much less biting into them!). "I like eating clams," said the boy from Barrington. "They're my favorite food."

A Most Unusual Double Play

Every summer, millions of kids flock to Major League baseball stadiums for a chance to see baseball played at its very highest level. And many of those same kids will bring along their trusted baseball gloves, hoping against hope to catch a foul ball off the bat of a real major league batter.

In August of 2009, C.J. Ramsey of Cedar Hill, Texas was one of the many hopefuls who happened to bring his fielder's glove to Rangers Ballpark one hot Sunday afternoon. Sitting high up in the bleachers behind third base, C.J., the boy's father, and also his uncle settled into their seats to enjoy nine innings of play between the Boston Red Sox and the hometown Texas Rangers. That is, the Ramseys and more than *30,000* other baseball fans.

Before those nine innings were over, 12-year old C.J. would become involved in one of the most unusual "double plays" ever witnessed in a big league park. The fun started while C.J.'s dad left his seat to buy some munchies at the nearest food concession stand. The Rangers' all-star outfielder, left-handed power-hitting Josh Hamilton, stepped in to face the Boston pitcher. Hamilton got an outside fastball, swung, and lofted a high foul pop behind third base. Up, up, and UP.

The ball sailed towards a surprised C.J., who said to himself, "Oh gosh, this is coming." Fighting off a man who was seated in the row just behind and to the right of C.J., the Little Leaguer reached as high as he could and snagged the ball out of the air. It was a difficult and rather athletic catch. C.J. immediately received a round of applause from fans in the upper deck. As television cameras zoomed in, the Rangers' announcer made a comment about how that's why it's a good thing to bring your glove to the park. "He's got a moment in time that he will never forget," observed the broadcaster, speaking about young C.J.

C.J., admiring the ball for a second, quickly handed the ball to his uncle.

C.J.'s uncle teased him about getting ready — just in case slugger Hamilton happened to send another foul ball streaking their way.

Meanwhile, C.J.'s dad, who had just finished purchasing a hot dog, heard the applause and looked up at the scoreboard monitor in time to see the replay of C.J. spearing the foul ball off the bat of Josh Hamilton. "Wow," said Mr. Ramsey. "How cool is that? C.J. just caught a foul ball!"

Then slugger Hamilton stepped back into the batter's box to resume his at-bat.

Moments later, there was another roar from the crowd, only this time much louder. Again, Mr. Ramsey checked the monitor, and again he got a glimpse of C.J. catching a ball. But something didn't seem right to Mr. Ramsey. Then, suddenly, it hit him.

This was a different catch. That's why the crowd was cheering so wildly. That's why they were giving C.J. a standing ovation!

C.J. had caught not one, but *two* foul balls — in the same inning and from the same batter, basically back-to-back.

How freaky is that?

One statistician calculated the odds of C.J.'s unique "double play" at just over three million to one.

C.J., who's been playing baseball since the age of four, now has two more special items to add to his prized collection of baseball trophies and awards. And in case someone doesn't believe C.J. about catching two fouls in a row, he's got the video and recorded television interviews to prove it. The Rangers even made C.J. that Sunday's "Fan of the Game."

Yep, two foul balls from the same hitter. That's a *three million-to-one* shot!

Not terribly bad odds if you happen to be a treasure kid.

Cape Cod Boy Recovers Treasure in the Grossest Place

Okay, so this next story is pretty gross. But it demonstrates how treasure can be found in the most unlikely of places — and at the most unlikeliest of times!

One spring day in 2008, 10-year old Cameron Delonde of Chatham, Massachusetts was simply minding his own business, brushing his teeth at the bathroom sink. The toothbrush somehow slipped out of Cameron's hand and, uh oh, bounced right into the toilet and slid down out-of-sight. Knowing that leaving a toothbrush there to clog the toilet might be a bad thing, Cameron got on his knees and reached way down inside to fish it out. Yuck! But while feeling for his lost toothbrush, Cameron also felt something else . . . something small, hard, smooth, and metallic. When he pulled his hand back out, the boy found himself staring at a pair of sparkling diamond rings!

Cameron gave the rings to his father. Mr. Delonde, with the help of a local Cape Cod real estate agent, was able to track down the former owners of the house. It seems that some twelve years earlier, two years before Cameron was even born, a Mrs. Mary Trainor had, in preparation for scrubbing that very same bathroom, removed her diamond rings and placed them inside a piece of toilet tissue to keep them safe. However, while busy cleaning, Mrs. Trainor accidentally knocked the rings into the toilet without knowing it, and then flushed. By the time Mrs. Trainor realized her big mistake, it was too late. The valuable rings were seemingly gone. Mrs. Trainor's adult son and daughter helped her search the toilet, but could not find the missing rings. The Trainors believed the rings had been washed into the sewer system and were gone forever.

Eventually, the Delonde family bought the house. Sadly, Mrs. Trainor passed away a few years later, and her son and daughter thought they would never see those precious rings again. But Cameron, whose hands were smaller than the adult hands which had searched the toilet years before, was able to successfully retrieve the lost treasure.

"To have the rings back is amazing!" said Mrs. Trainor's grateful daughter.

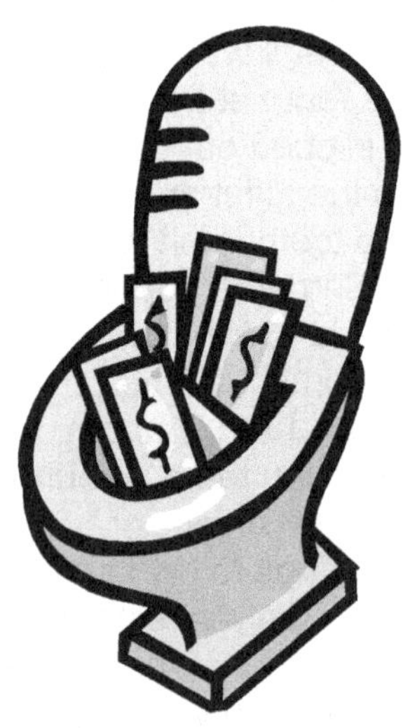

The Strange Case of the Meteorite Seven

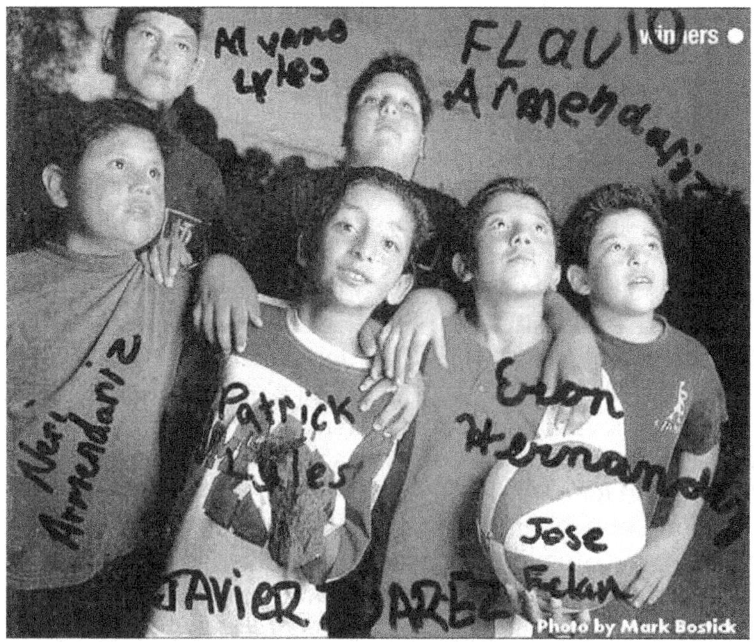

Source: www.meteoritestudies.com

Mr. Orlando Lyles was barbecuing in his Monahans, Texas back yard one spring evening in 1998 when a very curious event happened. Mr. Lyle's two boys, Alvaro, 11, and Patrick, 8, were playing basketball nearby with five of their neighborhood buddies when — BAM! —things got mighty interesting in a very big hurry. People at the barbecue and around Monahans, a town of 8,000 near Odessa and the New Mexico border, say they heard a series of four sonic booms. Those booms were followed by a strange whistling sound. Then, . . . **THUD!** A strange rock fell out of the sky, causing a dent in the empty lot between the Lyles' home and the home of their closest neighbor, Mr. Manual Juarez.

The seven boys playing basketball were nearest to the landing site, barely fifty feet away. The youngsters quickly gathered around the fallen object. Someone reached down and picked it up.

The rock was still warm.

Mr. Lyles called the Monahans Police. They arrived promptly, taking the mystery rock into custody and driving it to their police station. The next morning, a sheriff's deputy driving to work found another strange rock in the middle of yet another Monahans street. This rock had struck the asphalt so hard it was partially buried in the road.

Some smart-thinking police person called Evertt Gibson, a scientist with NASA's Johnson Space Center near Houston. Mr. Gibson caught the first plane he could to West Texas, retrieved the precious fallen rocks, placed them in plastic bags, and whisked the fresh specimens straight back to Houston for analysis.

Sure enough, the suspicious falling rocks proved to be meteorites. Stony or "chrondite" meteorites to be specific, from one large meteor that broke apart just before crashing to Earth in the western part of Texas.

Further NASA study of the meteorites, now called Monahans '98 I and Monahans '98 II, revealed a gigantic surprise. Using their electron microscopes, scientists in Houston were stunned to find evidence these space rocks contained very small traces of salty water, locked inside tiny bubbles called *inclusions*. Wow, water from space! Scientists were getting their very first up close and personal look at water not from this Earth. The tiny flecks of orange found on the rocks actually proved to be . . . *space rust*!

Meteorite experts claimed this valuable scientific find was possible because the boys had recovered their meteorite immediately after landing, and because NASA had gotten the two Texas specimens so very quickly.

However, back in Monahans, things were beginning to get a bit complicated. While our Meteorite 7 had become local celebrities, the space rock they had found was becoming increasingly valuable. Ownership of the meteorite was now in doubt. The empty lot between the Lyles and Juarez homes was actually public land. Some Monahans town officials were making noise that the meteorite called Monahans '98 I should be the property of the citizens of Monahans — all of them — not just the seven young boys who found it. Space rocks are big business in this day and age, with museums and collectors paying very big bucks for prized specimens. Rare and unusual meteorites, like the water-carrying Monahans '98 I and II, are often more valuable per ounce than even gold!

Countless meteors strike the Earth's atmosphere (becoming shooting stars), but only a small fraction of these, perhaps 500 per year, actually make it to the Earth's surface without burning up completely. Ones that survive the fall are called *meteorites*. Most space rocks fall in the ocean, out in the desert, up in the mountains, in forests, and onto other uninhabited areas — or at night when no one sees them. For someone to witness a meteorite strike the ground is an especially rare and fortunate event. Since most meteorites usually look much like ordinary Earth rocks, if no one sees them crash, they can often lie around unnoticed and undiscovered for thousands of years.

Lucky for our Meteorite 7, cooler heads eventually won out, and an excellent deal was struck for *all* involved. It seems way back in 1938 another meteorite was discovered near Monahans, buried in the sand hills 14 miles southeast of town. The 1938 iron meteorite, known as the Monahans Meteor, had since become the property of Arizona State University. Arizona State agreed to swap their 1938 meteorite for a large piece of Monahans '98 II, the one found by the sheriff's deputy smashed into the road surface. City workers actually dug up the patch of road where Monahans '98 II was discovered, and added that to their display. The city exhibit contains the valuable 1938 iron Monahans Meteor, a sizable fragment from Monahans stony '98 II, and the very scary impact crater dug out from the city street.

So whatever happened to Monahans '98 I, the meteorite that interrupted Mr. Lyles' barbecue and his sons' basketball game? The City Council of Monahans voted unanimously to return Monahans '98 I to our Meteorite 7. The famous boys from the Meteorite 7 are:

- **Flavio Armandariz, 9**
- **Neri Armandariz, 12**
- **Jose´ Felan, 11**
- **Eron Hernandez, 10**
- **Javier Juarez, 9**
- **Patrick Lyles, 8**
- **Alvaro Lyles, 11**

Using an Internet meteorite broker, the now-famous space rock was put up for international auction by the boys' families. The winning bid? A Big Spring, Texas businessman named Mike Craddock paid **$23,000** for the historic meteorite.

Just for playing basketball, waiting for some of Mr. Lyles' barbecue, and for being in the right spot at the right time, each of our Meteorite Seven collected over $3,000 (minus a fee to the meteorite dealer who arranged the sale to Mr. Craddock). Yes, paid thousands each just for a space rock that fell out of the sky, like money from heaven.

You could definitely say that was a slam dunk for the Monahans Meteorite 7!

Last Day of Summer Camp

Do you remember what you did on your last day at summer camp? Alec Burchick of New Port Richey, Florida's certainly remembers. July 31, 2009 is a day Alec Burchick, who was nine years old on that day, will never forget.

Alec had attended summer camp at the Jay B. Starkey Wilderness Park in New Port Richey, and was taking a nature walk down the Blue Bird Trail with friends he had met that month. The youngsters were looking for animal tracks, bugs, snakes, turtles — anything of interest.

"Something caught my eye in a pile of rocks," Alec explained. The piece of stone looked odd, out-of-place, somehow different than the other ordinary rocks. So Alec picked up the specimen and pocketed it.

Later, Alec showed the weird, pointy stone to Ms. Katie MacMillen, the camp's recreational later. Ms. MacMillen, realizing the stone was definitely of value, in turn called a local amateur archaeologist, Dr. Burton Golub (who is a dentist when not searching for artifacts). Dr. Golub, after conferring with expert colleagues at St. Leo University, announced that Alec's find was a type of ancient weapon known as a Newnan spear point. Now, how lucky is that?

Even better yet, based on the style of workmanship, where it was found, and the type of stone used to make the point, the archaeologists determined this particular spear point was approximately 6,000 years old.

"People took a lot of time to make these. It's a nice, what's left of it," observed Dr. Golub. Some Stone-Age hunter would have lovingly and painstakingly worked the original stone, chipping and flaking the material until the handiwork was razor sharp and ready for action. The point Alec found appears to have what archaeologists call a "contact break," meaning it was likely lost during a hunt when it struck bone or some other hard part of a large animal.

"When Dr. Golub told me it was 6,000 years old, I was so surprised I was close to crying," admitted Alec, who had recently finished fourth grade at local Longleaf Elementary.

Dr. Golub and the archaeologists at St. Leo's believe the delicate spear point was made during what is known as the Middle Archaic period. This was a time when nomadic wanderers were beginning to settle in larger numbers and put down roots in ancient Florida. Alec's find represents another piece in the ever-changing jigsaw puzzle that archaeologists are piecing together for a more accurate picture of the Sunshine State's distant past.

Mrs. LuAnn Burchick, Alec's mom, is just glad Alec took the stone to Ms. MacMillen. She says otherwise, the archaeologists wouldn't have identified the Newnan point, and Mrs. Burchick probably would've thrown out the specimen "while cleaning Alec's room."

The 6,000 year old artifact is now on display at the Jay B. Starkey Wilderness Park's education center. The park is crediting their 9-year old visitor with the excellent find.

Dozens of people, both kids and adults, walked that trail every day, but it was Alec's keen eye and strong curiosity that enabled the precious Newnan point to be recovered.

"It was an awesome experience," noted Alec, who has plans on one day becoming an archaeologist.

Source: *Tampa Bay Times*

World's Most Sensational Treasure Cave

Treasure Kids!

The last story in this book describes what may arguably be called history's ***best*** all-time discovery made by kids. In fact, it has often been described as the *greatest* archeological find in all the 20th-century. Not just by kids . . . but by anyone!

We take you back to southwestern France in the year 1940, during the very early days of World War II. Four French teenagers decided to join forces to search the oak forest just south of their village of Montignac. There was local legend about a long-lost tunnel that ran underneath the river from the Castle of Montignac to the Manor at Lascaux. And, supposedly buried somewhere in that tunnel, lay a fabulous treasure. The school boys, Marcel Ravidat, Jacques Marsal, Simon Coencas, and Georges Agnel, were determined to find those legendary riches and bring them home.

With the four exploring the woods south of Lascaux, Marcel's dog, a terrier named Robot, suddenly sprinted ahead. Robot chased an animal, either a rabbit or a fox, down into a hole hidden in the side of a hill. Covered by vegetation, this hole seemed quite small, resting as it was at the bottom of a depression caused by the roots of a long-gone fallen tree.

The treasure-seeking boys had some unexpected trouble retrieving Robot from the hole. Surprisingly, when they poked their arms into the tiny entrance, their fingers couldn't feel a bottom . . . only empty air. Next, the teens dropped stones through the opening to more accurately gage the hole's depth.

"Wow, this is a cave!" announced Marcel, who at 17 acted as the group's leader.

The boys decided to return days later, supplied with a few tools, some sturdy ropes, and a homemade oil lantern. Using pocketknives to widen the opening, the boys carefully lowered themselves down a surprisingly long vertical shaft covered with pointy stalagmites.

This was no doubt a cave — and a very big one.

"The descent was terrifying," recalled Jacques Marcel, who at 14 was the team's youngest member. But after lowering themselves down the nearly vertical 45-foot drop, the teen explorers entered a large rocky chamber about 100 feet long by 40 feet wide. Nervous, but no doubt urged on by thoughts of buried treasure, the boys crossed the darkened room by the flickering light of the oil lamp. There, the great room gave way to a narrow passageway.

Raising the lamp for a better look, the boys were now stunned by what they saw.

Animals floated across the surface of the next cave wall . . . multi-colored creatures that danced lifelike in the deep shadows, moving as they were somehow alive. Breathless, the boys pressed forward, discovering even more chambers and more rooms, the walls and ceilings of each covered with more dazzling paintings! Bison, bulls, deer, horses, bright red cows, big cats . . . even an animal that looked much like a unicorn The paintings were stunning, breathtaking, almost unbelievable, and far too many to count.

Promising to keep their incredible find a secret, the boys used hands, feet, and elbows to shimmy back up the dangerous vertical shaft. But this bold, brash promise would simply not be kept. The find was too enormous, the temptation to talk too great. One by one, each boy told other friends, escorting them secretly into the woods to explore the irresistible, exotic subterranean cave that lay hidden there.

Finally, it was Marcel Ravidat who sought the advice of Leon Laval, the boys' schoolmaster. At first, the wary teacher refused to believe his pupil, assuming this to be some sort of juvenile trick to make him look foolish. Or, worse, a brazen scheme to push the schoolmaster down an empty hole!

But when Marcel persisted, curiosity got the better of Monsieur Laval. And once the boys' teacher descended into that long-forgotten cave and got his first peek at the multitude of rich, colorful paintings, his initial skepticism turned to outright shock.

"Once I arrived in the great hall accompanied by my young heroes," said the French schoolmaster, "I uttered cries of imagination at the magnificent sight that met my eyes!"

Mr. Laval was immediately certain the more than *600* paintings and *1,400* etchings were prehistoric. He begged the boys not to let anyone touch the paintings, and to guard the new-found cavern from vandals. Indeed, young Jacques Marsal would make it his life's mission to defend and protect what would become known worldwide as the "Lascaux Caves." Jacques soon pitched a tent and began living at the cavern's entrance.

News quickly spread of the boys' fantastic discovery. Visitors swarmed to Lascaux to witness the sensational caverns. One visitor, explorer and scientist Abbe Breuil, known to many as the "Father of Prehistory," verified the ancient artwork to be *16,000* to *17,000* years old.

Chaos would soon sweep across France, however, as the Nazis invaded and occupied the country and much of Europe. Desperate times call for desperate measures, and the French Resistance, for a time, used the Lascaux Caves to store weapons in the struggle against their oppressors.

After World War II, Lascaux became a moneymaking tourist destination under the Count of LaRochefoucault and family, on whose land the caves had been uncovered. By 1948, as many as 1,000 people visited the caverns on a daily basis. Steps were installed for easy access, and Lascaux discoverer Jacques Marsal often led the tours.

By the 1960s, unfortunately, it became obvious the regular crush of humanity passing through the microclimate of the caves was doing great harm to the paintings. People breathe, and the warm carbon dioxide they exhale greatly increased the temperature and humidity of that fragile space. Condensation began to form on the caves' walls and ceilings, droplets threatening the very existence of vibrant prehistoric paintings people were paying to see. Germs and dirt tracked in on visitors' shoes caused a variety of molds and fungi to begin growing on the surface of the priceless, irreplaceable artwork. Faced with possible destruction of the site, long considered a national treasure by authorities, the French government took action in 1963 to close Lascaux to the public.

Since the 1960s, expensive air conditioning and dehumidification systems have been installed at Lascaux in an attempt to halt further damage. Access to the caves is strictly limited to scientists with special permits issued by the government of France. A large fence now guards the property.

A few hundred yards away, a replica of the caves, known as Lascaux Two, has been constructed opened to the public. This attempt to recreate the caverns as found by Marcel, Jacques, Simon, Georges, and Robot attracts a quarter of a million visitors every year.

Many books have been written about the "miracle" at Lascaux, widely considered to be the "Sistine Chapel" of prehistoric artwork. Scientists believe the ancient people of Europe considered these caves as sacred, a special gathering place for worship and storytelling. The main subjects of the paintings are animals, although there are some curious human figures along with abstract designs. The more than 2,000 paintings and etchings give modern science many clues about the daily lives of ancient humans — as well as the landscape they inhabited.

Treasure Kids!

Lascaux provides a unique window into the minds of our cave-dwelling and cave-painting ancestors from the distant Paleolithic past. It tells us much about their dreams, fears, hopes, and imaginations — the way cave people saw and experienced the world.

And we owe the wonderful gift of Lascaux all to four adventurous, curious boys. . . . Marcel, Jacques, Simon, and Georges. . . .

As well as a frisky, rambunctious terrier by the name of Robot.

Treasure Kids!

Sources

Chapter One — We're In the Money!

Legend of the Lost Union Payroll

1. *Buried Treasures of the Appalachians: Legends of Homestead Caches, Indian Mines, and Loot from Civil War Raids* by W.C. Jameson, August House, 1991.
2. www.losttreasures.com/content/archives/ state-treasures-tennessee
3. www.losttreasure.com — *"Storm Uncovers Union Army Payroll"*

Kids Bring Home $98,000 in Mysterious Duffel Bag

1. www.nbc5i.com — "*Three Colorado kids who found $98,000 and turned it into police have been told they can keep it.*" August 12, 2005.
2. www.the denverchannel.com — "*Kids Find $80,000 in Cash in Duffel Bag . . . Police Believe Money May be Drug-Related.*" February 16, 2005.

Israeli Boy Unearths Coin Described in Bible

1. www.haaretz.com — "*Rare first century half shekel coin found in Temple Mount dirt.*" December 19, 2008 by Nadav Shragai and Haaertz Correspondent.

2. www.haaretz.com — "*Rare first century half shekel coin found in Temple Mount dirt.*" December 22, 2008 by Nadav Shragai.
3. www.breakingchristiannews.com — "*Boy Finds Half-Shekel from Temple Mount That Survived Destruction of Jerusalem in 70 AD.*" December 23, 2008 by Teresa Neumann.

Ohio Boys Chase Snakes, Find Cash Instead

1. "*Striking It Rich — Two Boys Find Treasure While Playing in West Akron in 1951.*" *Akron Beacon Journal* by Mark J. Price, May 24, 2010.
2. *"Boys Must Wait 30 Days to Claim $1,400 in Old Can." The Sandusky Register,* May 1, 1951.
3. *"Pet Snake Leads Boys to Treasure." The Mansfield News Journal*, April 30, 1951.

Boy Finds Rare Penny Worth $72,000!

1. http://www.coins.about./od/famousrarecoinprofiles/a/1943copper_cent.htm — *"The 1943-S Copper Penny Found by Kenneth Wing (Teenage Collector Finds Rare Coin in Circulation)"* by Susan Headley.
2. http://www.creators.com/lifestylefeatures/collectibles/peter-rexford/a-penny-says-1943-was-a-very-good-year.html — *"A Penny Says 1943 Was a Very Good Year"* by Peter Rexford, 2007.

3. *"Laguna Coin Collector Sells Penny for Over $100,000." The Orange County Register*, August 4, 2008 by Chris Daines and Kelli Hart

Viking Coin Hoard Unearthed by Nine-year Old Boy

1. www.thelocal.se (Sweden's News in English) — *"Nine-year Old Boy Finds Buried Treasure"* by Paul O'Mahony, April 28, 2008.
2. *"Swedish Silver: 9-Year Old Boy Finds $265,000 Medieval Treasure Trove." Spiegel Online International*, April 29, 2008.
3. www.news24.com/Africa/News — *"Boy, Grandpa Find Treasure"* April 28, 2008.

Chapter Two — Jurassic Finds

Seven-year Old Uncovers Extinct Bison Skull and Horns

1. *"Bradford Bison Returning to Sauk Prairie." Sauk Prairie Eagle*, May 12, 2009 by Jeremiah Tucker.
2. *"Bradford Bison Will Return to Sauk Prairie." Sauk Prairie Eagle*, January 26, 2011 by Jeremiah Tucker.
3. *"Boy finds 5,000-year Old Bison Skull — Now Called the Bradford Bison." Capital Times*, by Mike Miller, December 11, 2005.

Treasure Kids!

Jurassic Prints Revealed in the Sand

1. "*Dinosaur discovery: Boy spots rare, perfectly preserved 'Jurassic' footprints.*" *Daily Mail*, February 22, 2008.
2. "*Dinosaur Dreams Comes True for Boy.*" *The Telegraph*, February 23, 2008.
3. "*British Boy Spots Dinosaur Tracks.*" *United Press International,* February 23, 2008.

A Cat Named Thera

1. "*Family Canoe Trip Turns Up One Heck of a Cat.*" *Anchorage Daily News*, by Linda Billington, October 26, 1995.
2. "*Tests Show Fossilized Skull of Lion Dates Back 19,000 Years.*" Daily Sitka Sentinel, April 12, 1996.
3. Correspondence via e-mail with the officials at the Alaska Museum of Science and Nature at www.alaskamusuem.org.

Dutch Boy's Memorable Day at the Beach

1. "*11-year old boy finds original jaw bone of dinosaur.*" *China View*, editor Mo Hong'e, August 3, 2008.
2. https://vandadelgado.wordpress.com/my-influential-art-and-artists/dinosaurs-in-lourinha-portugal-home-town. "*Dinosaurs in Lourinha, Portugal (my home town),*" by Vanda Delgado.
3. http://china.org.cn — "*Boy finds original jaw bone of dinosaur.*" August 4, 2008.

Six-year Old Boy Discovers Bone From Winged Dinosaur

1. "Beachcomber, 6, finds rare dinosaur fossil." *The Telegraph*, by Charlie Deveraux, July 11, 2007.
2. *"Boy, 6, finds 120 million year-old dinosaur bones." Southern Daily Echo*, July 10, 2007.
3. http://news.bbc.co.uk/2/hi/uk_news/england/hampshire/6288970.stm "Boy finds extinct reptile's bones." July 10, 2007.

Russian Boy Makes Mammoth Discovery

1. Woolly Mammoth: Life, Death, and Rediscovery by Windsor Chorlton, Scholastic Reference, 2001.
2. "*A Mammoth Excavation*" in *WebCurrents, January 11, 2010.*
3. www.russianlife.com — *"Jarkov Mammoth"* by Linda DeLaine, October 18, 2005.

Chapter Three — Golden Boys

Tale of the Baltimore Treasure Trove

1. Treasure in the Cellar, by Leonard Augsburger, The Maryland Historical Society, 2008.
2. "*Gold Comes Out of the Cellar and Into the Lore." The Baltimore Sun*, by Frederick N. Rasmussen, September 28, 2008.

3. http://www.uselessinformation.org/baltimore/index.html — *Baltimore's Buried Treasure.* Original Podcast Air Date: March 15, 2014

Gold Coins in Can Spark Montana Legal Feud

1. *"Trouble over a Treasure — "A Boy Finds $1,000 and Several Lawsuits Result." The New York Times,* September 2, 1898.

Brothers Discover Gold While Cleaning Henhouse

1. Treasure in the Cellar, by Leonard Augsburger, The Maryland Historical Society, 2008.
2. *"A Can of Gold in the Henhouse." Mail Tribune,* by Bill Miller, March 17, 2013.
3. Reports of Cases Decided by the Supreme Court of the State of Oregon, Volume 44, by Robert G Morrow, J.R. Whitney, Stine, 1904.

Teen Finds Huge Gold Nugget

1. *"Teen Strikes Gold at California Lake."* United Press International, August 6, 2008.
2. "*Teenager's Gold Nugget Find Could Spark New Gold Rush.*" KNBC Los Angeles, August 6, 2008.

3. *"Gold Fever Strikes — Discovery of Gold Nugget Brings Traffic to Foothills." Colfax Record,* by Dori Barrett, August 13, 2008

Iowa Boy Digging Form Worms Finds Fortune in Gold

1. "Iowa Boy Finds $50,000; Gold and Paper Money in a Box Buried in Clinton, Iowa." *The New York Times*, October 30, 1897.

Beep, Beep, Beep!

1. *"Three-year Old Boy Finds $4M Pendant in England." CBS Evening News,* November 18, 2010.
2. *"Boy, 3, unearths £2.5m treasure trove on FIRST metal detecting expedition." The Daily Mail* by Andrew Levy, November 17, 2010.
3. *"Boy, Three, Strikes Gold with Metal Detector." Sky News Online* by Kat Higgins, November 17, 2010.

Chapter Four — Treasure Girls

Girl Finds 2.93-Carat Diamond at "Finders Keepers" Park

1. *"Girl, 13, finds 2.93-carat diamond by path after day of fruitless digging." NBCNews.com, Associated Press,* June 7, 2007.

2. *"Missouri Girl Finds2.9-Carat Diamond in Arkansas Park." Fox News*, June 7, 2007.
3. *Teen Finds 2.93 Carat Diamond at National Park." Digital Journal* by WICCANIA, June 7, 2007.

A Girl and Her Saber Tooth Cat

1. www.nps.gov — *"Kylie's Fossil Find."* National Park Service web site under Badlands National Park.
2. www.wsbtv.com — *"Metro Atlanta Girl makes Major Fossil Find."* WSB-TV in Atlanta, June 29, 2010.
3. *"Saber Tooth Cat Fossil Undergoes CT Scan." Lakota Country Times,* February 2, 2011.

Fifth-grader Finds Rare Dragonfly

1. *"Rare Bug Caught by Texas Fifth-Grader." United Press International,* November 6, 2006.
2. *"Girl Finds Bug that's Rare for S. Texas." Corpus Christi Caller Times,* by Israel Saenz, November 6, 2006.
3. *"Amazon Darner (Anax amazili) Comes to Kleberg County." Argia, The news Journal of the Dragonfly Society of the Americas, Volume 18, Number 3,* October 26, 2006 by Tom Langschied.

Treasure Kids!

An Unexpected Treasure in Paradise

1. "Girl Returns $1,000 Found in Richard Simmons Tape." *USA Today*, October 29, 2008.
2. "Girl Turns in $1,000 Found at a Thrift Store," The Associated Press, October 30, 2008.
3. *"Girl, 11, Turns in $1,000 Found at Salvation Army Store." The Honolulu Advertiser* by the Advertiser Staff. October 28, 2008.

First-time Fossil Hunter Uncovers Ice Age Rhino

1. *"Five-year-old discovers Ice Age woolly rhino at first fossil hunt."*
   Daily Mail by Daily Mail *reporter*, November 5, 2008.
2. *"Five-year-old discovers remains of 50,000-year-old rhinoceros."*
   The Telegraph by Richard Savill, November 4, 2008.
3. *"Five-year-old unearths Ice Age rhinoceros bone." Express*.co.uk by Emily Garnham, November 6, 2008.

Money from Heaven

1. Rocks from Space, by Richard Norton, Mountain Press Publishing Company, 1998.

2. *'It Came From the Sky!' The Meteorite That Mangled the Malibu."* *The Daily Beast* by Michael Daly, February 17, 2013.
3. www.nyrockman.com — information on web site of R.A. Langheinrich Meteorites.

Ninth-grader Discovers Rare Supernova

1. www.astronomy.com — *"Profile: Youngest person to discover a supernova"* by Daniel Pendick, June 22, 2009.
2. *"Warwick girl, 14, is astronomy star: discovers a supernova in outer space." Times-Herald-Record* by Matt King, November 23, 2008.
3. *"New York Teen Finds Wimpiest Supernova." Sky and Telescope* by Valerie Daum, June 12, 2009.

Chapter Five — Amazing Adventures

Before Indiana Jones

1. *"London Lad Unearths Treasure in Backyard." The Daily Illini*, October 19, 1928.
2. *"Unearths Treasure in His Backyard," The Plattsburgh Sentinel,* October 5, 1928.

Treasure Kids!

Kids with Metal Detector Make Unexpected Find

1. *"Kids Finds Artifacts with a Metal Detector Their Parents Bought Them." Calvert Independent* by Matthew Vermillion, 2006.

History in a Bottle

1. *"Boys' Discovery Helps Archaeologists Form Better Picture of Area's History." The Washington Post*, by Ann Cameron Siegal, December 1, 2008.
2. www.marylandarchaeology.org — *"Virginia boys find history in a bottle." Newsletter of the Archeological Society of Maryland*, by Ann Cameron Siegal, March 2009, Vol. 35, No.3.

Ten-year Old Helps Solve Crime, Collects Reward

1. The Family, by Ed Saunders, Thunder's Mouth Press, 2002.
2. *"Boy, 11, Found Tate Murder Gun, Had Hard Time Convincing Police." Long Beach Independent Press-Telegram* by Mary Neiswender, September 4, 1970.
3. *"Boy Tells Tate Jury of Finding Gun." The Chicago Tribune,* September 5, 1970.

Treasure Kids!

Like Taking Candy from a Gangster

1. *"Dallas families live in fear after children uncover large cash stash." The Seattle Times* by Tanya Eiserer and Tawnwell D. Hobbs, January 29, 2005.
2. *"Dallas Students Threatened by Dealers to Return Found Drug Money." Dallas Morning News* by Tawnwell D. Hobbs and Gretel C. Kovach, January 27, 2005.
3. *"Dallas neighborhood worried after kids find pile of cash." The Item* by Jamie Stengle, Associated Press writer, January 30, 2005.

Searching for Sediba

1. *"2 Million Year-old Fossils Offer Look at Human Evolution." The Los* Angeles Times by Thomas H. Maugh II, April 9, 2010.
2. *"New Hominid Species Discovered in South Africa." The New York Times* by Celia W. Duggar and John Noble Wilford, April 8, 2010.
3. *"9-Year Old Kid Literally Stumbled on Stunning Fossils of a New Hominid." Discover Magazine* by Andrew Moseman, April 8, 2010.

World's Greatest Treasure Hunt Ever!

1. www.unmuseum.org — *"The Mystery Pit of Oak Island"* by Lee Krystek, 1998.
2. www.oakislandtreasure.co.uk — *"The Discovery of the Oak island Money Pit"*
3. The Secret Treasure of Oak Island, by D'Arcy O'Connor, Globe Pequot Press, 2004.

Chapter Six — Dynamite Discoveries

Young Hiker Discovers Ancient Indian Artifact

1. *"Teen Hiker Finds Rare Prehistoric Bowl."* NBC News, by *The* Associated Press, September 29, 2009.
2. *"Teen Finds Mogollon Artifact." Las Cruces Sun-News* by Levi Hill, September 30, 2006.
3. *"High School Student Makes Important Find, Then Demonstrates Excellent Archaeological Skills."* Southwest Archaeology Today, October 2, 2006.

Mystery of the Lost Ladybugs

1. www.lostladybugs.org — *"Welcome to the Lost Ladybug Project"*
2. *"In Search of the 'Lost Ladybug.'" The Los Angeles Times* by Tina Susman, April 23, 2012.
3. *"Ladybugs Lost." World Report* by Vickie An, May 1, 2009 Vol. #14 Issue #26.

Treasure Kids!

Georgia Boy Picks Up One Weird Space Rock!

1. *"Boy finds rare meteorite along Savannah River." Athens Banner-Herald* by *The Associated Press*, June 5, 2000.
2. *"Boy finds rare space rock." The Augusta Chronicle* by Robert Pavey, June 4, 2000.
3. *"A Tektite From Richmond County, Georgia." Lunar and Planetary Science XXXI*, 2000.

Blue vs. Pink

1. www.weau.com — *"Kids Find Rare Blue Crayfish."* July 12, 2006.
2. www.upi.com — *"Rare blue-eyed cicada creates a buzz."* June 12, 2007.
3. *"11-year-old boy finds pink grasshopper." The Telegraph* by Richard Savill, September 11, 2009.

No Ordinary Rock!

1. *"Boy, 6, gains honor for stone tool, 6,000; Artifact discovered in Sebasticook Lake." Bangor Daily News* by Sharon Kiley Mack, November 2, 2006.

Kids Use New Technologies to Make Discoveries in Space

1. *"Science students get stars in their eyes." The Washington Post* by Eric Niiler, October 4, 2010.
2. www.nrao.edu — *"West Virginia Student Discovers New Pulsar."* The National Radio Astronomy Observatory, January 19, 2010.
3. www.universetoday.com — *"Students Find Rare 'Recycled' Pulsar"* by Nancy Atkinson, February 2, 2011.

Chapter Seven — Lost and Found

Boy Finds a Bundle Bagging Groceries!

1. www.komonews.com — *"Integrity pays Federal Way teen who returned money,"* by KOMO staff and Associated Press, December 5, 2008.
2. *"Teenager turns in $10,000 cash he found in store." The Santa Fe New Mexican* by Steve Maynard of McClatchy Newspapers, November 27, 2008.
3. www.king5.com — *"Teen finds $10,000 at work."* KING 5 News, September 21, 2009.

Treasure Kids!

Boy Scout Recovers Purse with 19 "Benjamins"

1. www.npr.org — *"Boy Scout Returns Stolen Purse With $1,900 Inside."* National Public Radio, December 17, 2009.
2. www.nbcnews.com — *"Boy Scout returns purse with nearly $2,000."* Associated Press, December 16, 2009.
3. *"Boy's Football Hero Recognizes His Good Deed." News & Record* by Dioni L. Wise, December 29, 2009.

Fifth-grade Girl Hits Home Run with World Series Ring

1. *"Chatham girl helps return World Series ring to rightful owner." The Newark Star-Ledger* by Sarah Schillaci, May 7, 2010.
2. www.mlb.com — *"Girl finds, returns '60 World Series ring."* Pittsburgh Pirates web site on MLB.com by Alden Gonzalez, May 7, 2010.
3. nbcnewyork.com — *"11-Year-Old Returns 1960 World Series Ring"* by Erika Tarantal and Erica Butler, May 7, 2010.

Adopt a Highway, Take Home a Treasure

1. www.carolinalive.com — *"NH boy finds, returns backpack with $8K in cash."* The Associated Press, May 7, 2009.

2. *"NH boy picking up litter finds, returns backpack stuffed with $8,000 cash." The Gaea Times,* May 8, 2009.
3. *"Boy finds, returns backpack of cash." The Arizona Daily Sun*, May 7, 2009.

Toddler Recovers Precious Lost Jewelry

1. www.witn.com — *"Toddler Solves Three-Decade Old Ring Mystery."* November 7, 2009.
2. www.xenophilius.worldpress.com — *"3-Year-Old Boy Digging in Yard Finds Rings Lost 33 Years Earlier."* November 13, 2009.
3. www.generationbeta.com — *"Treasure in Your Own Backyard!"* November 12, 2009.

Treasure Girl Rides Summer Surf

1. *"Swimmer's Lost Treasure Returned." The Pittsburgh Post-Gazette*, August 26, 2008.
2. www.wpxi.com — *"Girl Finds Pittsburgh Man's Money, Credit Cards at Beach in Ocean City."* August 26, 2008.
3. www.foxnews.com — "Girl, 11, Finds $1,000 Floating in Ocean." The Associated Press, August 25, 2008.

Chapter Eight — Serendipity

Boy Discovers Rare Pearl — without Even Trying!

1. *"Lucky boy finds a pearl in his linguini."* The *Providence Journal* by Mary Murphy, 2009.
2. www.internetstones.com — *"Connor O'Neal Pearl."*

A Most Unusual Double Play

1. www.mlb.com — *"Young fan catches back-to-back foul balls"* by Lisa Winston, August 17, 2009.
2. www.nbcmiami.com — *"Young Rangers Fan Snags Two Foul Balls in a Row,"* by Scott Crisp, August 17, 2009.
3. www.bustedcoverage.com — *"Odds of Josh Hamilton Hitting Two Foul Balls into C.J. Ramsey's Mitt? 3.3 Million to One!"* by Joe Kinsey, August 18, 2009.

Cape Cod Boy Recovers Treasure in the Grossest Place

1. *"Long-lost rings found in toilet,"* by United Press International (UPI), June 30, 2008.
2. www.sndgems.com — *"Boy Finds Missing Rings in the Toilet,"* by Alex Miller
3. www.neatorama.com — *"Diamond Rings Found in Toilet . . . 12 Years Later!"* by Miss Cellania, July 1, 2008.

Treasure Kids!

The Strange Case of the Meteorite Seven

1. *"Monahans' meteorite seven learn lessons from 15 minutes of fame." Lubbock Avalanche-Journal* by the Associated Press, February 18, 2002.
2. The Fallen Sky by Christopher Cokinos, Thacher/The Penguin Group, 2010.
3. www.lpi/.usra.edu — "The Monahans, Texas Meteorite Fall of March 22,1998." By H. Povemire, 61st Annual Meteoritical Society Meeting.

Last Day of Summer Camp

1. *"9-year-old from New Port Richey finds rare 6,000-year-old spear point on nature walk." The Tampa Bay Times* by Michele Miller, August 9, 2009.

World's Most Sensational Treasure Cave

1. The Secret Cave — Discovering Lascaux by Emily Arnold McCully, Farrar, Straus and Giroux, 2010.
2. www.time.com — *"LIFE at Lascaux: First Color Photos from Another World"* by Ben Cosgrove, May 21, 2014.
3. www.savelascaux.org —*"Finding Lascaux — Four Boys and a Dog."*

(Page left intentionally blank)

About the Author

Jack Myers was born and raised in Philadelphia. He is the author of several books including *Row House Days*, *Row House Blues*, and The Delco Files. Jack has worked as a teacher, newspaper reporter, newspaper editor, pizza shop proprietor, and technical writer. In his spare time Jack is very active in the pet rescue community. He currently resides in Chester County, Pennsylvania and works for a Fortune 500 financial software company.

*** **If you liked this book, or have critical comments of a worthy nature, please post a review on Amazon!** ***

Jack's latest book is **Knights' Gold**.

Knights' Gold tells the amazing but true story of how two Baltimore boys in 1934 unearthed **5,000 gold coins** hidden by a secret Confederate organization known as the Knights of the Golden Circle. These millions of dollars in gold coins represent the largest documented K.G.C. treasure find yet!

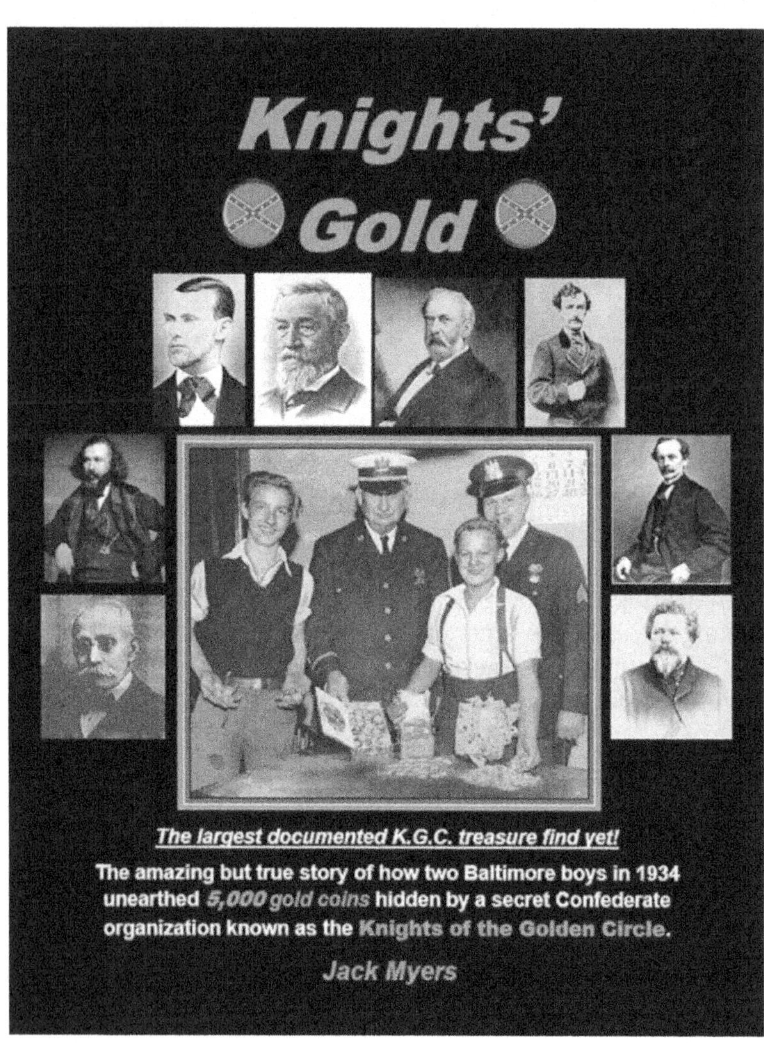
Knights'
Gold
The largest documented K.G.C. treasure find yet!
The amazing but true story of how two Baltimore boys in 1934
unearthed 5,000 gold coins hidden by a secret Confederate
organization known as the Knights of the Golden Circle.
Jack Myers

Made in United States
Orlando, FL
12 February 2022

14744885R10117